pring 2016

Mission

We understand "community literacy" as the domain for literacy work that exists outside of mainstream educational and work institutions. It can be found in programs devoted to adult education, early childhood education, reading initiatives, lifelong learning, workplace literacy, or work with marginalized populations, but it can also be found in more informal, ad hoc projects.

For us, literacy is defined as the realm where attention is paid not just to content or to knowledge but to the symbolic means by which it is represented and used. Thus, literacy makes reference not just to letters and to text but to other multimodal and technological representations as well. We publish work that contributes to the field's emerging methodologies and research agendas.

Subscriptions

We are pleased to offer subscriptions to CLJ—two issues per year:

Institutions & libraries	$200.00
Faculty	$35.00
Graduate students & community workers	$20.00
International Shipping	$10.00

Please send a check or money order made out to the University of Arizona Foundation to:

John Warnock, *Community Literacy Journal*
445 Modern Languages Bldg., University of Arizona, P.O. Box 210067
Tucson, AZ 85721
Info: johnw@u.arizona.edu

Cover Art

Photograph: "Words as/and Found Objects in the Desert Cityscape," by Adela C. Licona

Adela C. Licona's photography captures surface and depth. with camera in hand, she studies facets, textures, colors, patterns, & forms at times to document and at times to interrogate the mundane. she approaches her object photography as well as her eco-scapes, arte urbano/city-scapes, and body-scapes as "assemblages of stories so far." through a developed intensity in focus, her photographs often invite deeper inspections of the everyday. her work, referred to as "contemplative" and "queer" and noted for its depth as well as its "delicacy & intimacy," often explores interstices, propinquities, blurred boundaries, & bent light. as artist, scholar, & public rhetor, she is interested in provoking & participating in new ways of seeing & looking — reorientations, meaningful distortions, & re/visionings that are informed by — and might also inform — radical re/imaginings of being, belonging, and relating to one another, to everyday objects & everyday-scapes, to histories & bodies, to places & practices, and to the earth. See also: http://www.u.arizona.edu/~aclicona

Editorial Advisory Board

Jonathan Alexander	University of California, Irvine
Nancy Guerra Barron	Northern Arizona University
David Barton	Lancaster University, UK
David Blakesley	Clemson University
Melody Bowdon	University of Central Florida
Tara Brabazon	University of Brighton, UK
Danika Brown	University of Texas–Pan American
Ernesto Cardenal	Casa de los Tres Mundos, Managua
Marilyn Cooper	Michigan Technological University
Linda Flower	Carnegie Mellon University
Diana George	Virginia Tech University
Jeff Grabill	Michigan State University
Laurie Grobman	Pennsylvania State University
Greg Hart	Tucson Area Literacy Coalition
Shirley Brice Heath	Stanford University
Tobi Jacobi	Colorado State University
Lou Johnson	River Parishes YMCA, New Orleans
Paula Mathieu	Boston College
Regina Mokgokong	Project Literacy, Pretoria, South Africa
Ruth E. Ray	Wayne State University
Georgia Rhoades	Appalachian State University
Mike Rose	University of California, Los Angeles
Tiffany Rousculp	Salt Lake Community College
Cynthia Selfe	The Ohio State University
Tanya Shuy	U.S. Department of Education
Vanderlei de Souza	Faculdade de Tecnologia de Indaiatuba, São Paulo
John Trimbur	Worcester Polytechnic Institute
Christopher Wilkey	Northern Kentucky University

COMMUNITY LITERACY *Journal*

Editors	Michael R. Moore
	DePaul University
	John Warnock
	University of Arizona
Senior Assistant Editor	Amanda Gaddam
	DePaul University
Assistant Editors	Mariana Grohowski
	Massachusetts Maritime Academy
	Alexandra Nates-Perez
	DePaul University
Design & Production Editor	Ekram Othman
	DePaul University
Copy Editors	Jake Dinneen
	DePaul University
	Brandon Haskey
	DePaul University
	Mark Lazio
	DePaul University
	James Neisen
	DePaul University
	Margaret Poncin
	DePaul University
	Bridget Wagner
	DePaul University
Journal Manager	Daniel James Carroll
	DePaul University
Book & New Media Review Editor	Jessica Shumake
	University of Arizona
Social Media Editor	Janel Murakami
	University of Arizona
Consulting Editors	Eric Plattner
	DePaul University
	Stephanie Vie
	Fort Lewis College
	Maria Conti
	Univerity of Arizona
	Janel Murakami
	University of Arizona

spring 2016

Submissions

The peer-reviewed *Community Literacy Journal* seeks contributions for upcoming issues. We welcome submissions that address social, cultural, rhetorical, or institutional aspects of community literacy; we particularly welcome pieces authored in collaboration with community partners.

Manuscripts should be submitted according to the standards of the *MLA Handbook for Writers of Research Papers*, 7th ed. (New York: MLA).

Shorter and longer pieces are acceptable (8–25 manuscript pages) depending on authors' approaches. Case studies, reflective pieces, scholarly articles, etc., are all welcome.

To submit manuscripts, visit our site—communityliteracy.org—and register as an author. Send queries to Michael Moore: mmoore46@depaul.edu.

Advertising

The Community Literacy Journal welcomes advertising. The journal is published twice annually, in the Fall and Spring (Nov. and Mar.). Deadlines for advertising are two months prior to publication (Sept. and Jan.).

Ad Sizes and Pricing

Half page (trim size 6X4.5)	$200
Full page (trim size 6X9)	$350
Inside back cover (trim size 6X9)	$500
Inside front cover (trim size 6X9)	$600

Format

We accept .PDF, .JPG, .TIF or .EPS. All advertising images should be camera-ready and have a minimum resolution of 300 DPI. For more information, please contact Michael Moore: mmoore46@depaul.edu.

Copyright © 2016 *Community Literacy Journal*
ISSN 1555-9734

Community Literacy Journal is a member of the Council of Editors of Learned Journals

spring 2016

COMMUNITY LITERACY *Journal*

Spring 2016
Volume 10 Issue 2

Table of Contents

Articles

1   "If I Can't Bake, I Don't Want To Be Part of Your Revolution":
CODEPINK's Activist Literacies of Peace and Pie
Abby M. Dubisar

19   Lifting the Lid:
How Prison Writing Workshops Shed Light on the Social Shadow
Erec Toso

27   Challenging How English Is Done:
Engaging the Ethical and the Human in a Community Literacies Seminar
Susan Weinstein, Jeremy Cornelius, Shannon Kenny, Muriel Leung, Grace Shuyi Liew, Kieran Lyons, Alejandra Torres, Matthew Tougas, and Sarah Webb

43   Interview with Steve Parks
Jennifer Hitchcock

Book & New Media Reviews

57 From the Book & New Media Review Editor's Desk
Jessica Shumake
Saul Hernandez and Ryan Cresawn, Interns

59 Keyword Essay: Place-Based Literacies
Rosanne Carlo

71 *Writing Our Way Out: Memoirs From Jail*
Edited by: David Coogan
Reviewed by: Maria Conti

75 *Toward a Literacy of Promise: Joining the African American Struggle*
Edited by: Linda A. Spears-Bunton and Rebecca Powell
Reviewed by: Anthony Dwayne Boynton, II

"If I Can't Bake, I Don't Want To Be Part of Your Revolution": CODEPINK's Activist Literacies of Peace and Pie

Abby M. Dubisar

Abstract

By focusing on the cookbook *Peace Never Tasted So Sweet*, this article argues that CODEPINK strategically combines peace activist and food literacies to engage audiences in their antiwar efforts, strategies that take on benefits and drawbacks. Although feminist scholars from a variety of disciplines have studied cookbooks, researchers have yet to fully analyze the intersections of gendered activist literacies and cookbooks. Expanding upon arguments promoting food literacies as well as feminist analyses of cookbooks, this article illuminates CODEPINK's efforts to teach readers how to critique military action, recruit peace-workers, build a movement, *and* bake pie.

Food and food discourses hold persuasive power, a notion well understood by teachers who use food themes in their rhetoric and writing classrooms. Veronica House, for example, argues that teaching food themes is an essential act of civic literacy since the world food system is in crisis and educators thus have an obligation to engage students with the intersections of food, environmentalism, and sustainable futures (5). Cookbooks can also be understood as literacy artifacts that represent communities. Contributors to *Recipes for Reading: Community Cookbooks, Stories, Histories*, for example, address narrative elements in community cookbooks (Bower) as well as how the language of recipes defines communities (Cotter). Beyond classroom contexts, activists leverage political arguments by connecting them to food. Understanding such activists' rhetorical strategies helps literacy educators better appreciate how learning about food facilitates other types of learning in public spaces, paralleling the lessons about social justice aided by food literacy for students in House's courses.

Analyzing the 2010 cookbook *Peace Never Tasted So Sweet: Women's Delicious Recipes for a Sweeter World (With Action 'How-tos' and a Few Cookies Thrown in for Good Measure)* showcases peace organization CODEPINK's activist literacies. Examining their complex, potentially subversive gender performance linked to their literacy practices illustrates the intersections of cooking, gender, and peace. Known for both enacting and subverting gender norms in a wide variety of contexts and public performances, CODEPINK embeds multiple strategies in the space of this one text. As this analysis will illustrate, CODEPINK's cookbook takes on a number of tasks: subverting expectations in place for a cookbook by enacting political messages that connect food and peace, exploring gender's relationship to war, highlighting competing discourses about food, and showcasing ongoing feminist tensions between radical and domestic literacies. I ultimately argue that CODEPINK's cookbook strategically combines methods for engaging with peace activism and directions for preparing food in order to engage audiences in their antiwar efforts. Along the way my analysis uncovers how these strategies also take on benefits and drawbacks.

Food studies scholars have persuasively argued for the inclusion of food in classroom spaces and their justifications illuminate food's many cultural values and persuasive possibilities. Introducing the special issue on "teaching food," *Transformations* guest editor Deirdre Murphy draws upon existing food studies scholarship to note that in addition to the growth of the interdisciplinary food studies field, "the pedagogies of food demonstrate that our experience and analysis of selfhood, the natural and built environment, society, culture, and politics all filter through our engagement with the food we buy, grow, hunt, serve, cook, bake, or eat" (19). Building on these justifications for teaching food and the pedagogical possibilities of understanding food learning as a literacy practice, analyzing an activist cookbook enhances teachers' and students' knowledge on how combining food literacies with activist literacies can be accomplished in the genre of a cookbook.

As this study will show, women peace activists access and utilize diverse platforms to mobilize their messages and negotiate the meanings of food by publishing cookbooks. In such fruitful discursive spaces, women peace activists negotiate gender constructions to creatively articulate public arguments for peace and gendered motivations for mobilizing against war. The metaphor of a cookbook offers a framework for literacy and learning, as authors have titled their texts "cookbooks" whether teaching readers such diverse literacies as how to write code for computing, understand biomedical science, or engage in actual cookery.

For those engaging in literal cookery and producing cookbooks with organizations like churches and other groups, cookbooks communicate the values and priorities of a community. Rosalyn Collings Eves, for example, studies African-American women's cookbooks, arguing that they function rhetorically. The cookbooks exist to "memorialize both individuals and community [and] to generate a sense of collective memory that in turn shapes communal identity (281). Writing about online cooking websites, Elizabeth Fleitz also identifies community values from both single- and group-authored sites and understands single recipes as community texts, connecting such communal discourse to gendered literacy. Fleitz understands the writing of cooking as a gendered practice with a long history, arguing:

> Because women's literacy was devalued, women had to develop a new, useful literacy that would permit their communication practices to continue while

fulfilling the duties of their gender role. This type of literacy needed to be adaptable, with the ability to create and sustain strong networks of women. Thus, because of gender constraints, women developed literacy practices that relied on a variety of modes, creating flexible, open texts which are dialectic in nature and work to maintain bonds with others in the community. (4)

Resonant with Fleitz's observation, CODEPINK literally mixes the cooking literacies expected in a traditional cookbook with instructions on activist actions and strategies, pushing the boundaries of the genre while strategically utilizing a text available to women and tapping into a growing network of women activists.

Food as a Peace Issue

Food and peace come together in a long tradition started generations before CODEPINK published their book, yet their twenty-first century take on this intersection reveals considerable meanings for scholars interested the cookbook genre as a mode of literacy and cookbooks as artifacts of a community, as well as the intersections of food, war, and peace. As the rest of this analysis will demonstrate, CODEPINK's 2010 cookbook, published in conjunction with Mother's Day, uniquely offers instructions for how to critique military action, recruit peace-workers, build a movement, *and* bake pie.

Throughout the history of peace activism, women have positioned food as a peace issue, whether addressing the prevalence of food insecurity as a weapon of war or characterizing the ways in which women's traditional role of preparing food accommodates gendered pro-peace performance. For example, reflecting on her peace work, Jane Addams, president of the Women's International League for Peace and Freedom and Nobel Peace Prize winner, saw food and women's affiliated roles as essential for peace. Drawing on her experience working with the U.S. Food Administration, she wrote, "I hoped to find some trace of woman's recognition of her obligation to feed the world and of her discovery that such a duty was incompatible with warfare" (144). Broadening her claim, Addams continued, "I firmly believed that through an effort to feed hungry people, a new and powerful force might be unloosed in the world and would in the future have to be reckoned with as a factor in international affairs" (146). Thus, women's traditional role as food authorities positioned them to play an active role in diplomacy. In Addams's estimation, women's performance of gender roles and domestic expertise in war came to fruition through food.

A generation later, New York members of Grandmothers Against the War armed themselves with buckets of cookies when they arrived at a Times Square military recruiting station to enlist, positioning their aged bodies as disposable, unlike those of young military recruits, their grandchildren, with long lives ahead of them. To make their argument that war defines bodies and lives as disposable, the women balanced the embodied icon of the non-threating, baking grandma with the direct confrontation of a protest. The women chanted, "We insist we enlist!" (Wile

14) as they occupied the recruiting station and drew a crowd, eventually arrested and removed.

Additional discourses that rely on food to argue for peace include other peace organizations' cookbooks that come before CODEPINK's and establish a small yet vibrant tradition of such cookbooks. Other books of this kind include the 1968 and 1970 volumes of *Peace De Resistance* by members of Los Angeles's Women Strike for Peace (WSP) and the 1973 Greenwich Village Peace Center's cookbook *Peacemeal*. Often created for fundraising purposes, these cookbooks sometimes connect peace with baking specifically, as bake sales are traditional ways women can raise money for organizations and operate a gendered economy to support social justice causes. *The Great Day Cookbook*, for example, created by Velia Dean and Barbara B. J. Zimmerman of the Women's International League for Peace and Freedom, draws its title from the iconic quotation, "It will be a great day when our schools get all the money they need and the air force has to hold a bake sale to buy a bomber" (n. pag.). This quotation also reveals the power differential between militarism and peace, as one is massively funded and the other is not.

Although gender scholars beyond literacy studies have analyzed cookbooks, including history (Neuhaus), rhetoric (Eves, Fleitz, Hess, White-Farnham), communication studies (West), and popular culture (Bower), researchers have yet to fully consider the intersections of gendered antiwar activism and cookbooks nor the combined literacy promotion of cooking and activism. Scholars cannot have a robust understanding of women's peace activism literacies and their engagement with food without considering this genre.

CODEPINK's Deployment of Gendered Activism

To engage with the cookbook genre while also promoting their version of gendered antiwar activism, CODEPINK uses strategies that, on the one hand, position food as a peace issue and subvert expectations for gender norms, yet, on the other hand, take on the risk of sacrificing persuasive power in the interest of reifying the cookbook form and normative gender politics. Such inventive yet limited strategies further the tradition that CODEPINK established from their start, combining peace with gender performance, such as teaching strategies to actively reject the United States' practice of militarism with non-threatening practices like knitting.

Established in 2002, CODEPINK initiated its organization to stop the United States from invading Iraq. Since its inception, CODEPINK activists have performed a wide variety of rhetorical strategies to enact their causes. Addressing the readers of *Women's Studies Quarterly* in 2006, CODEPINK Coordinator for the New York City Chapter Nancy Kricorian writes of her organization, "You might have seen us around. We dress in pink and we make a ruckus" (532), succinctly summing up the rhetorical style and recognizable approaches the organization has become known for since their work began.

In an interview published in *Feminist Studies*, CODEPINK co-founder Jodie Evans accounts for her group's success in the immediacy and diversity of their strategies. She describes their approaches that build upon a number of tactics:

> The power of the visuals, the clear and powerful articulation of the message, the creativity, and the community of women. Being on the moment; when something happens we are there, with the research, with the direct connection to the human piece, with the humor, with the courage to be in places that are unexpected, bold, colorful, and speaking truth to power. Our actions inspire, they make people feel good, they bring people forward, they speak to the immediate, they take away the sense of powerlessness and move people into action, they also have hope and future in them. (Groves 200)

The role of community is essential to CODEPINK and the group's boundaries are porous; anyone can join. Likewise, their use of multimodal literacies aids their thorough and amplified broadcast of their ideas.

Studied by academics not only in expected contexts like women's studies (Kutz-Flamenbaum), but also in such diverse fields as law (Abrams), history (Moravec), international development (Milazzo), and media citizenship (Simone), CODEPINK both fits into the rich and long-standing tradition of American women's peace activism and the literacy events audiences expect such as delivering speeches, yet also invents new styles and strategies. For example, Kutz-Flamenbaum describes CODEPINK's strategic and accessible use of the color pink. At action events, established CODEPINK leaders make available pink colored clothing that new participants may take and wear in order to identify with the group and immediately become a part of an action, a wholly invitational strategy. Commenting on their ability to use multiple strategies at once, she writes, "The emphasis on women's role as pacifist caregivers presents a nonthreatening image of women activists... [reassuring] observers and new adherents that activists can be feminine and soft. Simultaneously, Code Pink's use of civil disobedience and aggressive trailing of public officials confound and challenge normative gender expectations of women as passive, polite, and well-behaved" (95). The cookbook also enacts this paired approach of nonthreatening femininity, the woman baker making tasty treats, with radicalism, the woman peace activist who is informed and forthright about military policy and spending.

Kathryn Abrams analyzes CODEPINK together with the work of California activist Cindy Sheehan and the antiwar movement Women in Black in order to understand how gendered citizenship is performed against war. Regarding CODEPINK, she writes of its incongruities and how they uphold multiple understandings of gender and women's power. According to Abrams, CODEPINK:

project[s] a paradoxical yet vehement image of citizenship: one in which improvisation aims at maximizing impact and reanimating politics; one in which proliferation, of activities and of personae, signals singularity of political will; and one in which exaggerated femininity—long read as the sign of apolitical triviality—is married to daring and committed public engagement. (852)

This very idea of flipping the expectations for apolitical triviality as a mark of femininity surfaces as a core feature of the cookbook, as the community cookbook originated as a gendered text. Thus, CODEPINK builds on that expectation that women write community cookbooks, yet subverts the cookbook's contents and persuasive potential.

Women's charity cookbooks that intervened in war launched the community cookbook genre. According to Food Studies scholar Andrew Smith, Maria J. Moss wrote her 1864 *Poetical Cookbook* to subsidize medical costs for Union soldiers injured in the Civil War (Stoller-Conrad). This origin of the communal cookbook is confirmed by Almagno, Reynolds, and Trimbur who write that Civil War "Ladies Aid Societies gathered recipes in collections to sell at fund-raising bazaars for war relief, instituting a longstanding tradition that links domestic recipes to women's public charitable work" (179). By the end of the nineteenth century, over two thousand such cookbooks had been published by charitable organizations, showing how popular such combined efforts of cookery and service had become (Almagno et al 179). Community cookbooks also became a vehicle for suffrage activists to promote their cause and raise money. A 1915 suffrage cookbook both connects food to political citizenship and calls for a pedagogy of eating when it declares:

> Eating and drinking are so essential to our living and to our usefulness, and so directly involved with our future state, that these must be classed with our sacred duties. Hence the necessity for so educating the children that they will know how to live, and how to develop into hale, hearty and wholesome men and women, thus insuring the best possible social and political conditions for the people of this country. (Kleber 7)

Eating well here is a national issue. Positioning women as professional nurturers who raise children with proper food education to ensure future national prosperity tempers the core issue at hand, women gaining the vote. In fact, because women must play such an essential role, enfranchising them through the vote fulfills full participation. Within this suffrage cookbook the issue of gendered peace activism surfaces as well. Mrs. Henry Villard, president of the Women's Peace Conference, issues a call to replace war's hatred, revenge, and cruelty with qualities that reflect "our" nature: compassion, gentleness, and forgiveness (Kleber 34). Following Villard's short essay is a photographic portrait of Jane Addams, who audiences are assumed to recognize since no biographical details are included. Both issues of suffrage and peace become connected in this suffrage cookbook that embeds political philosophy with its recipes, as the page following Addams's portrait is a recipe for Boiled White Fish.

CODEPINK continues this tradition with their cookbook, but positions it as a device that reflects their tailored and specific strategies. Here again the organization consistently uses gendered tropes to both subvert expected, normative feminine gender roles and engage accessible, gendered platforms. In the introduction to *Peace Never Tasted So Sweet*, CODEPINK founders Medea Benjamin and Jodie Evans position peace both as a social justice issue and an economic one, ripe for gendered intervention:

> To honor and embody Julia Ward Howe's original anti-war intention for Mother's Day, over the years we have gathered in parks and on beaches and bridges and in front of the White House to say "We, the women of one country,/Will be too tender to those of another country/To allow our sons to be trained to injure theirs." This year, not only will we be too tender—so will our pie crusts! We were inspired to create pies of peace after the 2011 US Federal Budget came out in February of this year and the United States military cut an unhealthy 48% piece of pie entirely for themselves and their wars. (Abileah and Hallock 1)

The introduction continues to pun on terms like "dough" that connect military spending and food, energizing readers to engage the book's lessons on activism by connecting them to baking. Thus, the cookbook format becomes a vehicle to disseminate activist strategies. In publishing their strategies under the guise of a cookbook, four themes emerge: the subversion of genre expectations for a cookbook by enacting political messages that connect food and peace, an exploration of gender's relationship to war, an intersectional featuring of competing discourses about food, and an embraced representation of ongoing feminist tensions between the radical and domestic.

Theme One:
Cooking up Peace By Subverting Gender and Genre

Peace Never Tasted So Sweet subverts expectations for a cookbook because it not only includes recipes for such pastries as "Lemon Cloud Pie" and "Chocolate Layer Torte," but also features conceptual recipes and instructions for organizing and taking action like "The Ultimate Recipe Peace Pie Party." The book itself is pink and the cover features photographs of women baking together and feeding one another, thus presenting the appearance of a cohesive yet diverse community of women. The individuals pictured include both children and adults, also representing an array of racial and ethnic identities.

While the written introduction immediately positions the book as a political document, the pie graph of U.S. budget priorities on the following page becomes the first evidence of the tools CODEPINK provides for its readers, as it features the proportions of money dedicated to the Pentagon, Iraq and Afghanistan military involvement, as well as the much smaller slices for veterans, health, education, justice, housing and other social needs. CODEPINK uses the pie chart as a call to action, stating, "To protest your money being spent mostly on war, call your congressperson, stop paying your war taxes, or follow the action recipes in this book!" (2). The first recipe, for peace parties, outlines the resources needed to host events that build partnerships and facilitate learning from one another for planning actions and political events, written in the form of a recipe with ingredients and step-by-step instructions. For new activists, such didactic material offers details for lessons learned by seasoned CODEPINK activists. The "recipe" suggests organizers can use social media to invite as many participants as possible, potentially hold a "peace pie bake sale," decorate the space with pink to affiliate with CODEPINK, provide food, and make people feel welcome. The recipe also provides the telephone number for the congressional switchboard so attendees can call their Congressperson "to ask her or him to stop funding war and bring their tax dollars home to communities in need… Don't worry if it's late. The switchboard will be operating and you can always leave a message for your Congressperson. Democracy never sleeps!" (5). The excited tone of this recipe for a gathering energizes readers when planning such an event may seem overwhelming.

Later in the book, another action recipe, for "radio pie," instructs readers on how to prepare for a radio interview. Contributor Josie Lenwell states that she always schedules an interview with a local talk show host in her hometown of Taos, New Mexico, within a week of returning from a CODEPINK event in Washington, D.C. Again building on food metaphors, the instructions indicate, "Most peace actions should be followed up by 'radio pie.' Your local radio station is often very hungry for hopeful and sweet news of the average citizen's quest for Peace and particularly hungry for a CODEPINK action for peace" (14). Readers may not consider radio as an effective outlet and also may not know that instead of waiting to be contacted for an interview, initiative is required to get the word out about their activist work and affiliation with CODEPINK. Thus, Lenwell's recipe outlines the details for pursuing this publicity venue. Lenwell's fifteen steps for preparing for and carrying out a successful interview showcase her rhetorical savvy and experience at engaging audiences. She directs readers to have their interview archived on the CODEPINK website to further broadcast their work and ends with the final step of celebrating interview success by eating a slice of a pie from the book (15). For new activists, a radio interview may seem daunting, but Lenwell's recipe invites readers to understand radio as a productive outlet, making the interview manageable and accessible so they can plan and prepare.

Another "action recipe" that offers communication strategies for engaging the public in antiwar work is Eva-Lee Baird's "phone-a-thon" pie. A member of the

Granny Peace Brigade as well as New York City's CODEPINK branch, Baird lists as essential ingredients an "easy-does-it phone script," a camera to record the action events and later post them to the CODEPINK website to publicize the action, a wide sidewalk busy with people, and bright explanatory posters to clarify for passers-by the engagement at hand. The leader of this action facilitates phone calls, using her own phone, between citizens and their senators and representative. As people walk by and view the signs about withdrawing troops and other peace messages, CODEPINK members invite them to use the available phone to make the call. Baird writes:

> This recipe works best during office hours. Callers are excited to speak to a live human in a Congressional office. *It will be a first time for most of the callers* and many will be nervous. You can hear *people overcome their hesitation* as they speak. By the end of the calls their voices will be stronger and more confident. They will leave with the resolve to call again. (54)

Baird boosts readers' confidence by not only offering these instructions that have worked well for her, but also encouraging them to not be shy.

Baird's work, and that of CODEPNK writ large, is to facilitate the peace activism of others and spread the desire to resist and enact change. In her introductory remarks, Baird quotes Burmese activist and Nobel Peace Prize winner Aung San Suu Kyi who believes, "when you are feel helpless, help someone" (53), framing the work of CODEPINK as encouraging others to take on the adventure and challenge of peace activism. Photographs of Baird engaging people on the street enhance this recipe, depicting a woman who initially appears surprised at the opportunity Baird offers her and represented on the next page talking on the phone and thus taking up Baird's offer. Furthermore, Baird's detailed instructions that include the timing for this practice thoroughly prepare others to host similar events. As a former teacher, Baird's recipe reads as a sort of lesson plan, paralleling the didactic forms of a recipe and teaching materials.

Other action pie recipes in the book cover effective ways to utilize social media, including how to write effective short messages, mastering persuasive storytelling, and identifying allies and targets; a recipe about building community through communication; and "disturbing the war pie," which positions activists to prepare for a congressional hearing on the department of defense budget. Submitted by retired Army Colonel Ann Wright, the "disturbing the war pie" recipe draws upon Wright's knowledge from serving in the military. A former U.S. diplomat, Wright resigned in March, 2003, in opposition to the invasion of Iraq, and has been arrested 15 times in protest of wars in Iraq and Afghanistan. The photograph representing her work features her facing government officials sternly, wearing a shirt that reads, "3800 dead. How many more" (49)? As these examples show, the genre of the recipe serves CODEPINK's purpose of inviting other activists to become a part of their transnational peace work, adopt their practices, and experiment with their strategies in new contexts, all justified in the context of a cookbook by relying on food tropes and recipe formats.

Theme Two:
Gender's Relationship with War

CODEPINK uses the book as a way to engage gender's relationship to war, a core tenet of their organization and its rhetorical strategies. Since their founding, CODEPINK articulates their gendered position, welcoming men while critiquing patriarchy's relationship to militarism. In the "About Us" section of their website, CODEPINK describes themselves as "women initiated" and positions their organization as a context for women to lead. After addressing the question "What is CODEPINK?," they attend to the question "Why women?" by articulating that "CODEPINK is not exclusively women—we invite men to join us—but we are particularly eager to see mothers, grandmothers, sisters, and daughters, female workers, students, teachers, healers, artists, writers, singers, poets and all outraged woman rise up and oppose the global militarism." Likewise, the prominence of women's leadership comes to fruition in the cookbook initially in the title, as the title phrase "women's delicious recipes" showcases the gendered authority the book features. CODEPINK dedicated *Peace Never Tasted So Sweet* to mothers in Afghanistan, Iraq, and other warzones around the world.

The organization thus hopes to unify women globally as they position all women in preventing war. Such unification is limited or mythical, however, since the cookbook is published in English and reflects most fully the experiences of privileged women who have the time and resources to compose a cookbook. This dedication and the cookbook as a whole also perhaps mask the extremely diverse array of women's experiences in war as well as peace activism. Regarding audience access to the text, a global, fully accessible engagement is impossible since readers must have an internet connection and the financial means to buy the book from publisher Lulu. com or other retailers.

That said, one recipe that furthers this international emphasis on women's roles in peace building is "Put a Smile on My World Cheesecake," submitted by Christine Hasan, Moona Fairooz, and "the kids at Rainbow for Kids Nursery" in the Kingdom of Bahrain, Arabian Gulf (42). In the recipe's introduction, the cheesecake is positioned as a mediator and creator of interpersonal harmony, as it "never ever fails to put a smile on even the angriest of faces." Following the recipe, a note includes the detail that Hasan and the children at Rainbows for Kids organized an International Women's Day event to promote peace in 2010, connecting their event to CODEPINK and Women for Women International. For their action, "Students made pink cupcakes and the women held up signs in Arabic and English saying, 'We are Women, Mothers and Sisters. We build bridges of peace every day. Join us in peace and understanding'" (53). With their recipe, action description, and photo of their action, Hasan and the children connect the nurturing work of a nursery with the global concern over war and peace-building, framing their roles of daily tasks of childcare with CODEPINK's mission to end war.

Another contributor, Lorene Zarou-Zouzonis, connects her recipe on the broader cultural tradition of women compiling recipe books. Excerpted from a cookbook written by Palestinian women living in Michigan, Zarou-Zouzonis's recipe for "Sfeeha, Meat Pie" facilitates her description of her family's immigration from Palestine to Detroit in the 1960s. A poet, fiction author, peace and human rights activist, and community organizer, Zarou-Zouzoni also has an activist daughter who visited the Gaza Strip with a CODEPINK delegation and later organized a larger student delegation. Thus, Zarou-Zouzoni's contribution not only features a gendered lineage of cooking and writing cookbooks, but also highlights CODEPINK's activist work as multigenerational (59).

Speaking to its diverse representation of connecting gender and activism, following Zarou-Zouzounis's Palestinian recipe is Diane Wilson's recipe for "Cajun Truck Driver's Shrimp Pie," a juxtaposition of food traditions and cuisines not likely found in any other cookbook. Wilson, a Texan, co-founded CODEPINK. A fourth-generation shrimper, Wilson became a boat captain at the age of 24 and continued in such work until she read about toxic pollution and her county's status as its number one producer. This moment prompted her lifelong dedication to environmental justice. Known for her many acts of civil disobedience, Wilson is also legendary for inspiring other women to take action in their communities and beyond (60-61). Such examples show CODEPINK's interest in connecting gender and antiwar activism and engaging with the question of what difference gender makes when layering the additional context of food and cooking on to the antiwar activist context. Further, due to the diversity of women featured, CODEPINK resists positioning gendered approaches to peace activism as singular, but instead publishes the recipes, perspectives, and biographies of women who carry out peace and gender in a wide variety of iterations.

Theme Three:
Food and its Meanings For Gender and Peace

As a third theme, the cookbook highlights competing discourses about food. Thus, just as diverse women submitted wide-ranging recipes to the book, a variety of approaches to food and meanings ascribed to food also surface in the cookbook. Such potentially conflicting definitions of a "good" recipe or "good" food reflect the ongoing ambivalence about food in mainstream American culture in recent years. For example, emphasizing locavore practices that highlight seasonal, whole foods can be critiqued as an elitist framework that rewards those with access to land and other material resources with purportedly the tastiest, healthiest food (Pollan). Like labels that use "organic" or other terms that position food as an alternative to conventional (potentially chemically-laden, toxic) foods, such designations can turn out to be meaningless or simply trendy. That said, some activists see alternative eating practices and avoiding corporate food as ways of enacting their beliefs and promoting social, environmental justice.

One "action pie" recipe specifically connects war to food production. Maria Bravo's contribution, "Mountain Apple Pie: A Recipe for Budding New Activists," directs readers to plant apple trees in their own back yards, without chemicals. After five years, when the tree bears fruit, Bravo encourages readers to bake a pie with fresh, organic ingredients. In the final step of the "recipe," Bravo writes:

> You will have so much fun taking care of your tree and watching the wildlife that you will probably want to grow more of your own food…If more people grew some of their food we would use less oil to ship our food around the country and therefore we would not need wars for resources. War kills many innocent people and animals as well as destroying the earth. (44)

Positioning food and its production as antiwar action again subverts the expectation for a cookbook, which requires ingredients for recipes and teaches techniques, but generally does not address how, where, and why to source food from various producers. Bravo encourages readers to buy apples from a local farmer if growing them is not possible, positioning so-called "locavore" practices as politically powerful.

While some people shun prepared foods, for activists and others most interested in saving time that can be dedicated to non-cooking justice work, prepared foods facilitate quick and accessible cuisine. Furthermore, since many of CODEPINK's members highlight their roles as mothers and caregivers who provide food for others, which involves a great deal of time and labor, they may even more strongly emphasize ways that food needs to provide accessible nutrition at a low cost, rejecting "foodie" culture's habit of endowing food with semiotic power as fetishized objects.

For CODEPINK contributors, these competing approaches to cooking and eating exist within the same cookbook. While Bravo's recipe asked bakers to grow their own apples without chemicals and bake a pie five years later when the apples have grown, other recipes such as "No-Bake Healthy Pie" require three immediately accessible ingredients: a prepared graham cracker pie crust, organic French vanilla yogurt, and fresh fruit (39). Poet contributor Dian Sousa also embraces prepared foods, as her recipe for "Pie Cakes" requires only a frozen crumb-top apple pie and one recipe of prepared pancake batter. To accomplish the recipe, cooks chop up the frozen pie and mix it into the pancake batter before making pancakes in the traditional way. Sousa suggests freezing leftover cakes to make ice cream sandwiches (33). Thus, food and cooking can take on many meanings for the cook-activists featured in this single book.

Other food traditions and approaches featured within the book are raw and vegan cooking, both positioned as potentially political eating habits that benefit health and personal well-being as well as environmental engagements that promote sustainability. Ariel Vegosen's recipe for "Raw Key Lime Pie" opens with her message: "I recommend using as many local, organic, and Fair Trade ingredients as possible. Avocado and coconut oils are great for you and this will leave you feeling satisfied and guilt-free!" (74). Since the recipe calls for macadamia nuts, coconut, avocado, agave nectar, and coconut oil, cooks using this recipe may feel baffled by where one would have to live to access such ingredients from local producers, yet the advice remains as a way to ideologically frame the values often affiliated with socially-conscious, health-focused eaters.

Such diverse food approaches and politics featured in the context of this single book make an argument for expanding and reflecting upon food's meanings. Obviously some of these approaches focus on fun and whimsicality, engaging cooks with their inventiveness. Others prompt readers to think about food systems, to consider how foods reflect nationalities and ethnicities, or position food as a way to engage others and make connections across personal boundaries. CODEPINK's cookbook makes a case for a much more intersectional look at food politics that takes into account diverse motivations and accessibility for cooks living in a wide variety of locations and under various material conditions. What may seem fractured in the cookbook's identity is actually an underlying argument toward expanding what it means to be a politically conscious eater and activist. The cookbook reflects the complex relationships between food, gender, and peace politics that a single approach to food cannot address.

Theme Four: Gendered Cooking's Radical, Domestic, and Feminist Tensions

Feminist tensions surrounding the political features of food preparation and other domestic tasks frame another significant theme, including implications of both domesticity and radical politics as sites of struggle. This intersection locates CODEPINK's cookbook in the context of the "new domesticity" movement that "reclaims" domestic tasks and roles, privileges "making," and upholds DIY approaches as marks of independence, self-sufficiency, and anti-corporate behavior. Of course such considerations are nothing new for CODEPINK activists, as they have always played with traditional and revolutionary notions of what it means to perform gender.

Quoted in the article title, CODEPINK includes on the back cover of the cookbook the declaration, "If I can't bake, I don't want to be part of your revolution." This position directly addresses tensions regarding feminism, activism, and gendered performance of domestic tasks. This tension has been taken up more recently by writers like Emily Matchar and others who examine the ideological power of "hipster housewives" who embrace both feminism and domesticity, positioning work in the home as the truly radical, progressive action. While women affiliated with

CODEPINK likely position themselves at similar places politically, Matchar points out how "new domesticity" and its DIY ethics writ large appeal to a wide swath of ideologies. Thus, Matchar's research points out how baking and cooking are flexible signifiers for gender representation. Speaking directly to this colliding discourse, Matchar quotes food philosopher Lisa Heldke:

> 'This movement can get claimed and co-opted or used by all these different people on different places on the political spectrum'...Heldke jokes that when she brings her homemade bread to a party where she doesn't know the guests, she has to explain who she is and what the bread means. As in, is she a conservative farmwife or a liberal neo-homesteader? Does the bread symbolize her identity as a modern woman or that she is her grandmother all over again? (214)

This need for gendered justification categorized by Heldke reinforces why CODEPINK uses baking as a way to invite new, perhaps younger, activists into their organization. For women and others, baking and cooking can hold many meanings. Gendered cooking performance, for CODEPINK, occurs outside of the heteronormative family, does not position women as remanded to domestic spaces, but instead operates as an invitational strategy to make events welcoming and get people to engage with the book and CODEPINK's ideas. Instead of feeding their families, as second-wave women were imagined to do in earlier peace cookbooks, CODEPINK bakers take their baked goods outside the home.

Because the cookbook never directly addresses how and in what ways baking itself is a radical act, however, it does run the risk of being marginalized as a cookbook only, not a radical political action book. Because the "action recipes" are the core materials of the book, their impact may be hidden within the undervalued context of a cookbook. For CODEPINK, baking is an entry point to a conversation and a way to showcase their activist work as accessible, exciting, and essential, but since cookbooks are historically marginalized as insignificant, domestic manuals, their peace mission may be covered by the emphasis on food. However, CODEPINK wants us to break free of this concern that activists cannot be taken seriously when they simultaneously write cookbooks, bake, and engage in radical peace activism.

Scholarship on women's peace activist cookbooks supports this notion. Isaac West, for example, demonstrates how "women are active agents capable of producing politically progressive identities even as they act within potentially problematic discursive circuitries" (361). In his study of two Vietnam-era cookbooks published by the Los Angeles branch of Women Strike for Peace, West concludes that "mothers who resist militarism *as mothers* by appropriating this interpellation can, and sometimes do, mobilize an important critique of the gendered logics of warfare and the proper role of women as citizens" (377). West's point can be extended beyond the identity of mother-authority to escape the dichotomy that women-identified activists have to decide whether to embrace the label of bakers or peace activists when also identifying as women. Thus, the liberal/conservative binary that Heldke characterizes must be deconstructed in order for both gender and peace progress to occur.

CODEPINK is also invested in destabilizing this binary of women as passive domestic workers *or* active political agitators who reject domesticity, as their cookbook takes as a given that women can, and must, take on both roles of peace activist and cook that harness all available means of persuasion. In many ways CODEPINK activists do not have time to attend to gender politics and trendy "new domesticity" explorations and critiques. Their insistence on immediacy, educating publics about military funding and policy, engaging social media, and representing themselves by documenting and broadcasting their activities shows how they cannot trust others to fully represent their work.

Ongoing Implications for Cookbooks as Gendered, Activist Literacy Artifacts

Reading CODEPINK's cookbook closely highlights both the affordances and limitations of the cookbook genre. While it may be too quickly dismissed as a marginal, minor, domestic text that positions the cookbook in undervalued contexts or pushes it to the periphery of peace activist texts, it is also an essential document for the organization. The cookbook facilitates CODEPINK's ongoing combination of gendered tropes with activist strategies and is thus a key method for engaging audiences and propelling their messages into all available spaces.

To imagine a continuing progressive tradition for cookbooks as activist discourses, cookbooks must continue to be understood and published as a collective genre that holds multiple meanings. Such flexibility for the genre would ensure an intersectional complexity that accommodates diverse and at times contradictory outlooks on the intersections of food, militarism, gender performance, and patriarchy. Ann Freadman's concept of genre "uptake" helps illuminate why CODEPINK and other organizations like it need the genre of the cookbook as a powerful discursive tool, one that works with other genres to promote change (39-52). Uptake highlights how genres interact with one another and thus do not exist in isolation. Citing Carolyn Miller's assertion that genres represent social action, Freadman reinforces how the dynamics of such social action reveal how genres get people to do certain things with one another (40). Thus, the thematic reading of CODEPINK's book featured here pushes on the possibilities for how a peace cookbook can operate as a literacy artifact and teaching tool when we understand it as one persuasive genre in a wide range of strategies the organization takes on to enact antiwar activism, recruit new members, describe group activities, and more.

As readers "take up" *Peace Never Tasted So Sweet* they experience a range of lessons beyond expectations for a cookbook. CODEPINK builds on the universal need to eat, the drive to cook, and the collective memory of cooking as a cultural practice in order to simultaneously promote activist literacies and their community values. By continuing to perform close readings of activists' use of various genres, subversive strategies, and intersectional gendered literacies, scholars can better understand how peace activism is evolving in the twenty-first century. Rhetoric and composition instructors especially can utilize texts like *Peace Never Tasted So Sweet* with students to showcase genre flexibility as well as how activists expand their communities through various literacy strategies. To reinforce House's call for instructors to fulfill the obligation of exposing students to food literacies and social justice, the time has never been better to facilitate learning about how social justice activists both instruct and initiate effective strategies.

Works Cited

Abileah, Rae and Whitney Hallock, eds. *Peace Never Tasted So Sweet: Women's Delicious Recipes for a Sweeter World (With Action 'How-Tos' and a Few Cookies Thrown in for Good Measure)*. Lulu.com, 2010. Print.

"About Us." *codepink4peace*. Web. 15 Oct. 2014.

Abrams, Kathryn. "Women and Antiwar Protest: Rearticulating Gender and Citizenship." *Boston University Law Review* 87.4 (2007): 849-882. Print.

Addams, Jane. *Second Twenty Years at Hull House: September 1909 to September 1929, With a Record of a Growing World Consciousness*. New York: Macmillan, 1930. Print.

Almagno, Stephanie, Nedra Reynolds, and John Trimbur. "Italian-American Cookbooks: Authenticity and the Market." *Popular Literacy: Studies in Cultural Practices and Poetics*. Ed. John Trimbur. Pittsburgh: Uni of Pittsburgh Press, 2001. 175-188. Print.

Bower, Anne L. "Cooking Up Stories: Narrative Elements in Community Cookbooks." *Recipes for Reading: Community Cookbooks, Stories, Histories*. Ed. Anne L. Bower. Amherst: Uni of Massachusetts Press, 1997. 29-50. Print.

_____. "Our Sisters' Recipes: Exploring 'Community' in a Community Cookbook." *Journal of Popular Culture* 31.3 (1997): 137-151. Print.

Cotter, Colleen. "Claiming a Piece of the Pie: How the Language of Recipes Defines Community." *Recipes for Reading: Community Cookbooks, Stories, Histories*. Ed. Anne L. Bower. Amherst: Uni of Massachusetts Press, 1997. 51-71. Print.

Dean, Velia and Barbara B.J. Zimmerman. *The Great Day Cookbook*. Quixott Press: Doylestown, PA: 1983. Print.

Eves, Rosalyn Collings. "A Recipe for Remembrance: Memory and Identity in African American Women's Cookbooks." *Rhetoric Review* 24.3 (2005): 280-297. Print.

Fleitz, Elizabeth. "Cooking Codes: Cookbook Discourses as Women's Rhetorical Practices." *Present Tense: A Journal of Rhetoric in Society* 1.1 (2010): 1-8. Web.

Freadman, Ann. "Uptake." *The Rhetoric and Ideology of Genre: Strategies for Stability and Change*. Ed. R.M. Coes, L. Lingard, and T. Teslenko. Cresskill, NJ: Hampton Press, 2002. 39-52. Print.

Groves, Sharon. "Interview with Code Pink Co-Founder Jodie Evans," *Feminist Studies* 31 (2005): 200-203. Print.

Hess, Marta. "Projects in the Making: Establishing Community and Identity in Junior League Cookbooks." *Peitho* 14.1 (2012): 1-6. Web.

House, Veronica. "Re-Framing the Argument: Critical Service-Learning and Community-Centered Food Literacy." *Community Literacy Journal* 8.2 (2014): 1-16. Web. 1 Dec. 2014.

Kleber, L.O. *Suffrage Cook Book*. Pittsburgh: The Equal Franchise Federation of Western Pennsylvania, 1915. Print.

Kricorian, Nancy. "CODEPINK Women For Peace," *Women's Studies Quarterly* 34 (2006): 532-533. Print.

Kutz-Flamenbaum, Rachel. "Code Pink, Raging Grannies, and the Missile Dick Chicks: Feminist Performance Activism in the Contemporary Anti-War Movement." *NWSA Journal* 19.1 (2007): 89-105. Print.

Matchar, Emily. *Homeward Bound: Why Women Are Embracing the New Domesticity*. New York: Simon and Schuster, 2013. Print.

Milazzo, Linda. "Code Pink: The 21st-century Mothers of Invention." *Development* 48.2 (2005): 100-104. Print.

Moravec, Michelle. "Another Mother for Peace: Reconsidering Maternalist Peace Rhetoric from a Historical Perspective, 1967-2007." *Journal of the Motherhood Initiative* 1.1 (2010): 9-29. Print.

Murphy, Deirdre. "Toward a Pedagogy of Mouthiness: The Essential Interdisciplinarity of Studying Food." *Transformations: The Journal of Inclusive Scholarship and Pedagogy* 23.2 (Fall 2012/Winter 2013): 17-26. Web. 4 January 2015.

Neuhaus, Jessamyn. "The Way to a Man's Heart: Gender Roles, Domestic Ideology, and Cookbooks in the 1950s." *Journal of Social History* 32.3 (1999): 529-555. Print.

Pollan, Michael. "Why Eating Well is 'Elitist.'" *The New York Times "On the Table" Blog*. New York Times, 11 May 2006. Web. 11 Nov. 2014.

Simone, Maria. "CODEPINK Alert: Mediated Citizenship in the Public Sphere." *Social Semiotics* 16.2 (2006): 345-364. Print.

Stoller-Conrad, Jessica. "Long Before Social Networking, Community Cookbooks Ruled The Stove." *NPR The Salt Blog*. National Public Radio, 20 July 2012. Web. 1 Nov. 2014.

West, Issac. "Performing Resistance in/from the Kitchen: The Practice of Maternal Pacifist Politics and La WISP's Cookbooks." *Women's Studies in Communication* 30.3 (2007): 358-383. Print.

White-Farnham, Jamie. "Rhetorical Recipes: Women's Literacies In and Out of the Kitchen." *Community Literacy Journal* 6.2 (2012): 23-41. Web. 13 Jan. 2014.

Wile, Joan. *Grandmothers Against the War: Getting off our Fannies and Standing Up for Peace*. New York: Citadel Press, 2008. Print.

Author Bio

Abby M. Dubisar is an Assistant Professor in the Department of English and affiliate faculty member in women's and gender studies at Iowa State University. She teaches courses in the rhetoric and professional communication program and program in speech communication.

Lifting the Lid: How Prison Writing Workshops Shed Light on the Social Shadow

Erec Toso

Abstract

While the social, political, economic, educational, and cultural consequences of high rates of incarceration have been well documented, the social psychological dynamics have not received as much discussion. I offer here a first person narrative reflection on the connections between a writing workshops and raising social awareness of the realities of day-to-day lives of inmates. Appropriate writing pedagogy, personal challenges to meeting to the workshops, and the need to publish inmate stories inform the essay.

When I point my old Subaru south, the familiar butterflies take wing. I drive toward the tracks, the coal-fired power plant, and the state prison, where I will meet the writing workshops. About the time I merge onto the interstate, I get nervous. The reasons are both trivial and close to a live nerve.

I am nervous that I will not do a good job running the workshops. That's the teacher in me, and my apprehension is well founded. The workshops have been going on for almost forty years, and they have a decorated, high-profile history. There is no way I can live up to what Richard Shelton has done with inmate writing—National Book Awards, Endowment for the Humanities grants, and on and on. But I am a teacher and writer and pay attention to the challenges in front of me, which loom large as I approach the Arizona State Prison Complex at the end of Wilmot road.

The "population" of workshop members is a Rubik's Cube of ethnic diversity, previous education, expectations, and attitudes toward writing. It's a challenge not unlike a tough English 101 class, but the racial divides and prison politics, the "shot-callers" and gang affiliations are all there, waiting at the door when the workshop is over, hanging over the yard like a poison cloud. I am not totally naïve about the realities of inmate life, especially in the higher security yards, yet even this is not the core source of my agitation.

I am concerned that I have not sufficiently prepared, that I have forgotten to type or make copies of inmate work, that I am not up to the job of providing what these men need to improve their writing. I feel some of the same butterflies on the first day of college writing classes for similar reasons. All teaching situations require customized planning, whether teaching upper-division nonfiction prose classes, first-year developmental writing, or prison creative writing workshops. I do not get nervous because I will soon be sitting in a room with twenty inmates in a medium-high security unit of the Arizona State Prison Complex, nor because of the sometimes rigid and byzantine bureaucracy that seems to be forever changing the rules. No, the nervousness comes from a fear that I will have to meet some of my own demons, that I will shrink from the harsh facts of inmate stories, that I will fail to help the men to tell their stories in a way that readers will find compelling enough to see the human face behind the words.

Yes, there is more going on here. Prison is more than a place of confined bodies; it is also, literally and metaphorically, the place of confined, broken, disowned, and silenced stories. It is no secret that the US has the highest documented rates of incarceration in the world, and Arizona ranks sixth among the states at 572 in prison per 100,000 residents. Much has been written about the social, political, and economic costs of incarceration, but the social psychology of American incarceration hasn't received much attention. There is more even than a kind DSM catalogue of mental illness and how prisons have become the holding bin for the mentally ill who have no advocates or resources. There is even a more subtle, more insidious, dynamic at work.

Prison reflects what Carl Jung calls the shadow, that aspect of the psyche to reject and disown the unpleasant aspects of a whole human. Unpleasant traits like addictions, poverty, mental illness, violence, racism, ignorance—the whole package—ends up locked away. What is "human" includes as much atrocity as it does fine art, after all. Jung contends that denying the shadow comes at a great cost, that vitality decreases in proportion to the energy needed to keep the shadow at bay. It is worth noting that he does not argue for acting out the "Mr. Hyde," aspects of the psyche, but that full autonomy results only from being aware of what is in the shadow, how it shows up in fits of anger, sadness, depression, even psychosis. He argues the "enlightenment does not come imagining figures of light, but my making the darkness conscious" (Jung). He also says that how the mind organizes itself manifests in social organization and behavior. What goes on inside, in other words, takes a parallel form outside, in social structure, institutions, organization.

One might ask, "How does darkness become conscious?" Good question that. The best way I know is through story. The disowned elements of the psyche rise to consciousness in dreams and story. Stories have a way of defusing some of the tension of repression, freeing that energy for creative work. Making art is another way to touch the shadow. Inviting inmates to create and—in the process—to access some of that shadow, is one way to make their presence conscious to the psyche of the free world, the un-incarcerated.

The inmates in our prisons are the exiled aspects of the social body, the rejects, the throwaways, the denied. Many of the men I work with in prison are there because they are the leftovers when opportunities ran dry. Society does not offer everyone the same chances, the same educations, the same encouragement or preparation. The ones who are left out of the legal avenues to upward improvement have no choice but to make their own opportunities in underground systems, black markets, organized gangs, or criminal taking of resources.

If I am honest with myself, I know that I am no better than they are, and, quite possibly would have made the same choices given similar situations. Yes, there are dangerous men in prison, violent sociopaths who should be contained. But there are others, many others. Nonviolent drug offenders usually make it in the workshops. I know some who claimed they needed to feed a family, so played the only game open to them; they did what they had to do. Being a product, in some ways, of my environment and privilege, I know that I did not have to make some of the choices these men made. Going into the prison reminds me of those parts of myself that I have not had to feed to survive.

I have to consider the truth of stories I would rather not hear and that those stories serve as witness for those unpleasant facts that the free world would rather ignore. It is my place to raise the questions that will lead to more effective telling: forms and quality that will result in publication. In many ways, I am the bad news that stories will have to rewritten if they will ever go beyond the privacy of a festering wound.

The butterflies settle as I pass through the six electric gates, three ID checkpoints, and the long walk across the open yard to the Programs Building. As the men enter the room and help to set up the desks and chairs, I find myself on more familiar ground, talking about language and ideas, the same topics I address in college writing classes. It is this point of contact, this negotiation, and how it differs between the prison and the university that I would like to explore. It's a good subject, and one that, as a teacher, I find challenging to think about.

When I first consider the differences in how I approach college classes compared to the prison workshops, I see more continuity than disconnect. In some ways, in other words, writing is writing, whether it be a freshman comp class at the university or a creative writing class in the prison. I am not surprised to eavesdrop on the men in the workshop at the door to our classroom arguing over the uses and abuses of profanity or whether explicit violence is necessary to develop a particular story. Inmates are often less jaded and more passionate about style and content than my undergraduate students, though both share the interest. All that said, the contexts and purposes of prison writing workshops and college writing courses are drastically distinct and require that I tailor methods and materials to fit the job.

The biggest difference between my university teaching and the prison workshops is what one could call the "social and political constructs" within which the writing happens. Angela Davis coined the term "prison industrial complex" as way to get a handle on the epidemic increase in incarceration along with the growth of private, for profit prisons (Davis).

Our prison population is the highest in the world, and part of what leads to incarceration is illiteracy. Learning to read and write makes it less likely that one will end up in prison, or, in the case of already being there, makes it less likely that an inmate will return. The reasons for decreased recidivism and literacy are not fully understood, but the relationship has been documented, and parsing the particulars is beyond the scope of this essay.

As a teacher, I need to understand the context of the workshops. Inmates don't get credit, grades, or degrees for their writing. Inmates come to the workshops for a wide variety of reasons, sometimes just to get some paper and a pen. More often than not, they bring some kind of question, something about how to express feelings they cannot contain, or an inquiry about how to compose a letter to a judge. Sometimes they come for the wrong reasons and find better ones as time and writing progresses.

The prison population, like any other, is diverse and complex. J., for example, graduated from an Ivy League school before becoming a heroin addict, and C. dropped out of school in the eighth grade. Yet they see themselves represented stereotypically in television, film, and advertising as lowlifes, cruel, mentally deranged, stupid, comically inept. As a result, inmates have desensitized to criticism or gotten so thick skinned that they accept it with much of a struggle. Paradoxically, they tell me the workshops are a place where they can feel, be more human for a while.

Inmates write about a world I barely know—one of addiction, homelessness, violence, prostitution, as well as love, hope, and spiritual life. They patiently explain terms like "tweaker" and strategies to stretch food stamps, like buying a cheap item with the stamp and then taking the cash for what they really want. They have few illusions about clichés like a fair, blind justice system and are jaded about equal enforcement of laws. Unlike students at the university, I do not have to persuade inmates that poverty, race, and class all figure in to opportunities offered.

Consider the work of J., an addict, a self-identified ex-member of the Aryan Brotherhood, and one of the more serious members of the workshop:

Heroin Cosmology

A flame flickers
Beneath the flimsy white plastic spork
But it does not melt
Into an unrecognizable blob.
Instead, thousands of tiny new planets
Sizzle into existence, pop into extinction
A fresh galaxy of euphoria.
The clear plastic mosquito slurps its fill
And the newest god winces
As the needle-sharp silvery fang punctures.
He begins to pray to Him
To see crimson swirling and congealing

Mixing with dark nirvana, however temporary
It is evidence of true aim.
As the smooth black rubber o-ring rams home
And the white circle of string
Is untied from above a bicep
Eyelids droop, jaws slacken, mysteries are revealed,
And A-H-H!
The vice tightens
Another turn
The grip
Like jaws of a leg-hold
Trap.

    J. grew up in Phoenix, lived on the streets after he dropped out of high school, and saw no hope of going to college. He was married for a while and has children. He is an Arizona son who is shrewd enough to see opportunities and take them.

    The physical space of the workshops is decidedly low-tech: no ELMO, LCDs, connectivity, or even overhead projectors. The workshops operate in the age of pencil and paper. Regimentation, martial authority, and predatory relationships pervade the yard. All of this adds up to a "no bullshit" atmosphere. My persona has to be one that radiates confidence and commitment to what we are doing. I have to believe in it. I have to have reasons that the inmates understand and respect for what we do.

    Writing in the workshops is intrinsically motivated. That is, I don't tell them what to write about. They choose the subjects, though I do give "assignments" for those who are stuck. For example, I might ask them to describe an idea or concept as a character, to personify an abstraction like despair. But I tell them that they have to do the assignment or something else that they want to work on. Most just work on what they want to write about. The work is usually what we composition people call "expressive" or creative—prose, poetry, and fiction, or some blend of them.

    The inmates bring a rich well of experience to the workshops but not always the technical skills to present that experience in a way that most readers will find interesting or comprehensible. In order to polish the writing, inmates must work on language, rhetorical strategies, syntax, form. We talk about matching the subject to the form best at conveying it. It is heady, hard work. The "lessons" of "showing, not just telling," using figurative language, selecting telling detail, and many others, are all woven into the context of drafting, revising, editing.

    Another aspect that contributes to motivation lies in the end goal of the workshop: publication. The Poetry Project is supported by a grant from the Lannan Foundation that pays for a yearly magazine. For years it was the *Walking Rain Review* under Richard Shelton, but now it is *Rain Shadow*, part tribute, part description of the meteorology around the prison.

    A literary journal speaks to a wider audience than most of the inmates write for. They write for each other, and the results are sometimes embarrassing in the sophomoric and puerile humor, the sexism, the scatological hilarity. When I point to this, often the only voice that wants improvement, they tell me I would understand if I were incarcerated. I don't disagree and remind them that they aren't just writing for other inmates if they want their work published. In order to publish, they have to move beyond complaining or the easy slapstick and find an image or a telling detail or a story with breathing characters rather than general abstractions. These are the messengers that both speak from the shadow and to a reader. Energy is exchanged and art is born. This, to me, is when the writing becomes truly dangerous in making connections between the free world and that of the prison.

Here is a poem from B., a long-time member of the workshops who has published regularly for over ten years.

Cut From The Will

Though you knew—
I know you knew—
I was already stuck outside
In the rock garden's far end
Atop a three-headed saguaro.

So, why?
I never could make myself
Eat a whole crow
But didn't I always bring each
Broken body to the backdoor?

I know you saw them.

I left them for you
There on the limestone stair
With its unshaped edge and map
Of dried mildew islands.

I saved you,
Saved you from your stone dream:
Brought you black feathers
Broken bits of wing and claw.
I left them—always—so
You could find them
Where the afternoon shadows

From the backyard's single cottonwood
Reach the door's sedimentary tread.
Open up!
You hear me,
I know you hear me.
Just open the damn door...
I'm asking...

They can try to publish anywhere, and they bring in drafts to workshop for science fiction magazines, travel magazines, literary magazines, and contests like the Pen America Prison Writing Contest.

In other words, the workshops are a means to an end of reaching an audience and not an abstract audience, but one that might pay for the right to publish.

Given that the workshops have limited seats and participants that self-select, most of the inmates want to learn, desperately in cases. They do not carry an inheritance of entitlement, like many of the undergraduates at the UA, however. Many come from families that did not expect high levels of literary attainment. They were not told to go to college, become doctors, lead. Many of the inmates have been homeless or addicted, or have grown up in abject poverty or dropped out of school. In terms of writing, many have trouble with spelling and punctuation and are not afraid to ask basic questions about nouns, verbs, sentences, or whether or not it is better to begin with a detail or a broad overview. They lean in sometimes to ask what a word brought up in discussion means. They want to participate, learn, inquire. Sometimes the profundity of the questions, such as what is a sentence or what makes a paragraph, leave me scratching my head because I don't know for sure. I can't define the difference between poetry and prose other than by vague generalizations. They make me think about the fundamental functions of language, the role of a sentence as the smallest unit of story, character, and action. They push me to question ways we dramatize the unspeakable.

Given that the context, population, physical resources, and motivations of the prison workshops differ so dramatically from the college writing class, what can a teacher/writer do? How do I negotiate this difference?

The first move I make is to meet them where they are, wherever that is. Then it is time to listen to what it is they need and what the best ways are to offer that. Some inmates need critique, sometimes sharp critique. Others may need encouragement, recognition for exploring difficult subjects or experiences. Sometimes the best thing I can do is listen. Some of them just want to have their say, to speak their truth, share a hard-won realization. These intangibles may be the reward of the workshops. Inmates get no direct social promotion for the workshops, but they can glean some better understanding of themselves by working on creative pieces.

When inmates join the workshops, their writing is often overly sentimental and distressingly abstract. They write, understandably, to daughters, girlfriends, and mothers in language more appropriate to Hallmark cards than to literary publication.

Or it is confessional, sensational, and graphic but goes little further than rendering scenes in distressingly harsh detail. They begin by recording experience, to the point where there is only circumstantial detail, with little or no broader audience appeal or larger idea. The next level of writing—which begins with a deep engagement with the subject—begins to examine a theme or idea and is a big step and depends in part on levels of reading, education, awareness of a worldview or vision. The bigger ideas, the context, the overlap with an outside reader's world seem unnecessary or unworthy of consideration. The learning curve for these men is steep. Sometimes, in a matter of months, they write with greater maturity, precision, and honesty. They hear, in the other men's work, real effort to capture experience through well-chosen, independent, fresh, well-earned language.

They have to grow beyond embryonic ideas of what good writing is and how much work it takes to shape and share a complex thought. I realize that I am talking to myself when talking to them. I see that what needs to be said in my own life is the hard stuff—my fears, anger, and sense of injustice. It takes so much energy to keep that repressed, bottled up, confined. I have begun that process but have not finished. There is work to be done. It begins with invitation, leads to listening, and then progresses to the craft of shaping for oneself and for a reader. It is one thing to be heard, another to be understood.

When I reload the Subaru and head back toward the city, I remember that when I began to write, I found someone inside myself I did not previously know. The words led to ideas, strung together an identity, spoke taboos, and affirmed beliefs. The words took on a life of their own when put to paper. They made some of the darkness conscious. It is the words wrung from darkness that I trust when I go to the prison or to the classroom. With some respect, skill, and something to say, students and inmates might find a way to save us from ourselves.

Works Cited

Davis, Angela. ""Masked Racism: Reflections on the Prison Industrial Complex." *Colorlines,* 10 Sept. 1998. Race Forward. Print.

Jung, Carl. *The Collected Works of C. G. Jung.* 1st ed. Vol. 13. Princeton University Press, 1967. 265. Print

Author Bio

Erec Toso teaches in the Writing Program at the University of Arizona. His first memoir, *Zero at the Bone – Rewriting Life After a Snakebite* was published in 2007. He was has published essays in *The Sun – A Magazine of Ideas, The Briar Cliff Review, Northern Lights,* and has published book reviews in *Rhetoric Review.* He runs prison writing workshops at the Arizona State Prison, Tucson Complex.

Challenging How English Is Done: Engaging the Ethical and the Human in a Community Literacies Seminar

Susan Weinstein, Jeremy Cornelius, Shannon Kenny, Muriel Leung, Grace Shuyi Liew, Kieran Lyons, Alejandra Torres, Matthew Tougas, and Sarah Webb

Abstract

Eight English graduate students and a professor reflect on their semester-long exploration of community literacy studies. The students, some in a MFA Creative Writing program and some doing doctoral work in literature, rhetoric, or English Education, discuss how the community literacies lens unsettled their relationship to English Studies.

Background

In 2008, Fero et al. published an article titled "A Reflection on Teaching and Learning in a Community Literacies Graduate course" in this journal about the experience of teaching and learning in a seminar on community literacy practices, designed for a new graduate concentration in Rhetoric and Writing at Michigan State University (82). A second case study, "Community Engagement in a Graduate-Level Community Literacy Course", appeared in *CLJ* in 2014, and described a seminar designed for a graduate program in Rhetoric and Technical Communication at Michigan Technological University (Bowen et al. 18). Each of these texts offered a model for the community literacy seminar, while also pointing to the particular challenges involved in connecting university programs and graduate students to community spaces.

When I contacted *Community Literacy Journal* editor Michael Moore in the summer of 2015 to ask about ways of connecting my planned Fall 2015 community literacies seminar to the journal's work, his immediate suggestion was to build on the work of Fero et al. and Bowen et al. by contributing a third seminar case study. This article, then, represents the results of that study and expands the dialogue by centering a seminar *not* situated within a Rhetoric/Writing/Communications program and *not* populated solely by graduate students studying under such a rubric. Researching Community Literacies, the course this article describes, took place at Louisiana State University in Fall 2015 within a traditional English department with a large literature concentration, a well-known MFA Creative Writing program, and a smaller concentration at the graduate level in Rhetoric, Writing, and Culture (RWC). The eleven student participants in the seminar came from across those concentrations—five were MFA students in either poetry or fiction, three were doctoral students in literature, and two were doctoral students in RWC. The class also included one PhD candidate from Education.

The present article asks what it means for community literacy studies to "travel" outside of writing studies, to be taken up by graduate students who want to explore what it would mean to engage with people and practices beyond the academy as a part of their work in creative writing, literary studies, queer studies, and postcolonial studies—some of the areas represented by the students in our seminar. What does it mean for community literacy studies, and what does it mean for a largely traditional, literature-centric university English program, for its graduate students to be invited into the distinct way of imagining scholarly and creative work that a study of community literacies engenders? To address these questions, and following a brief seminar description, the rest of this article is organized thematically. During our last class meeting in the fall, as each student described their research project, I took notes on the themes I heard coming up within and across presentations. I shared these back to the students, and we revised them together to create the format for the following sections. In each, one or more students reflect on the way the particular themes played out in their research.

Seminar Description (Sue)

LSU English is a large department in a research university that is also the flagship state university. It's the former home of the storied Southern Review literary journal, and literary studies—particularly southern literature—has long been central to the department's identity. Graduate students in the department focus on a range of areas within literature; rhetoric, writing, and culture (RWC); and creative writing, in which we offer a terminal MFA. The MFA is a three-year program requiring substantial academic study in English alongside writing workshops, so graduate seminars in English include a mixture of students, some pursuing the MFA and some the PhD.

My own research field is New Literacy Studies (NLS) (Gee, 1996; Street, 1985), which views literacy practices as always already ideological, and that, therefore, calls for studies of socially situated engagement with verbal texts that attend to the power dynamics inherent in those situations. Most graduate students taking my seminars are new to both NLS and to conducting research with human subjects, to use the clinical language of the IRB. My challenge is to offer a balance of material that introduces students to the field of NLS, while also leaving space to investigate a particular set of questions and for students to develop seminar projects that speak to their larger academic and creative interests.

The seminar that is the focus of this article took place in Fall 2015, and was titled "Researching Community Literacies." In the past, I have only attempted a methodological focus once in a seminar because the students come in with so little experience and because ethnographic methods are complex, varied, and require more than a single semester of study. Yet I knew we had a number of graduate students who wanted to get off campus and connect with community spaces. The syllabus that resulted attempted to do a few things: 1) provide an intensive orientation to qualitative research ethics; 2) offer an introduction to research methodologies; 3) trace a broad historical trajectory of literacy studies, including community literacy studies; and 4) include multiple and diverse examples of community literacy research. Since I had the good fortune to already know most of the students registered for the seminar, I selected readings that would skew to their interests, and this is a key way that the seminar differed from those described by Fero et al. and Bowen et al. While our early semester readings included two critical community literacy text, Elenore Long's *Community Literacy and the Rhetoric of Local Publics* and Higgins, Long, & Flower's "Community Literacy: A Rhetorical Model for Personal and Public Inquiry," we quickly branched out into a number of related but distinct fields that reflected the interdisciplinarity of our group. I chose to include readings from performance studies because it is a field that can serve as a connector between the qualitative and the literary/creative, growing as it does out of both the consciously heightened performance of theater and Erving Goffman's study of "the presentation of self in everyday life," to borrow the title of his 1959 book. Several articles from rhetoric and culture scholar Phaedra Pezzullo (2003a, 2003b) offered a useful author study for our seminar, given that one study took place in southeastern Louisiana and that much of her work reflects the complexities of participant-observation and of activist scholarship.

Despite some disciplinary departures from the two earlier seminars documented in *CLJ*, and specifically because most of the participants had no experience with either the field of community literacy studies or with researching with human subjects, our early class meetings took up the very questions with which the 2008 Fero et al. study begins:

1. What is a community?

2. What is literacy?

3. What, therefore, is community literacy?

4. What does it mean to practice community literacy—to write, to teach, to learn, and so on? (83)

Indeed, our first class meeting saw participants breaking into small groups to attempt an answer to those first two questions, brainstorming and recording ideas on large sheets of paper that we then posted and discussed at length.

The other major consideration for the course design was the research component. Cushman and Grabill, as the professors of the Michigan State seminar, opted not to require participants to conduct research in community spaces during the course of their seminar, but questioned that choice in the Fero et al. article:

> We thought carefully about this, but one of us (Jeff) was insistent—perhaps too insistent—that any work outside the university be linked to existing work and relationships. We did not want to send our graduate student colleagues forth to volunteer or design a study or engage in work that was not already part of an existing relationship. This made the course perhaps too conceptual in its conduct. […] Therefore, we left one key tension untouched—the tension between our often elegant theories of what communities are, what literacy should be, and how we ought to design our activities and the less-than-ideal realities of literacy projects. (90)

Designing her Michigan Tech seminar several years later, Bowen took heed of Cushman and Grabill's self-critique and required seminar students to participate in Breaking Digital Barriers (BDB), a volunteer-based community program with which Bowen was already involved. Her students split their time with BDB between working with program attendees and taking field notes for research. Ultimately, that research led them to design and facilitate several workshops in addition to BDB's regular offerings (21).

In Baton Rouge, I work with several community youth organizations, but none is structured in a way that would have allowed for all eleven graduate students to participate in a single program the way Bowen's students did with Breaking Digital Barriers. Each student in the LSU seminar, then, was required to identify a research project of their own involving a specific community of practice. This broadened the definition of community literacies from the strictly service-oriented to include practice-oriented spaces. Despite Long's hesitance around researching online communities (11-12), which seminar participant Sarah Webb takes up further on in this article, we chose to include digital communities as an option for research. This option was helpful given the wide variety of disciplines and fields of study among the seminar students, and also ensured that students who lacked experience with community service spaces and who might not be productive within those spaces could meet the course requirements while avoiding harm to themselves or others. I further attempted to mitigate risk by focusing the first several weeks of the semester on research ethics. Students had to complete the NIH training for conducting research with human subjects that LSU's IRB requires of its researchers, and we read several articles from Paris and Winn's *Humanizing Research: Decolonizing Qualitative Inquiry with Youth and Communities* (2013).

Finally, fresh off a week-long summer Critical Participatory Action Research Institute at CUNY Graduate Center's Public Science Institute, I encouraged students to consider forms of publication instead of, or in addition to, the traditional academic essay. While I acknowledge the continued primacy of the academic essay in English studies and do not want to hamper graduate students' chances on the job market, I am energized by the power of alternative forms of publication used by activists and artists in order to reach a variety of audiences and to reinforce the content of their work.

In the following section, seminar students describe and reflect on several elements of their experience researching community literacies. Following the overall purpose of this article, which is to consider how and to what extent community literacy studies can challenge traditional graduate English practices, we focus on themes of challenge: to our pre-existing assumptions about what academic research looks like and how it is conducted, to our understandings of our own positions in the various communities we inhabit, and to our sense of the purpose of scholarship in the world.

Thematic strands
Challenging pre-existing expectations

Alex: When I registered for the seminar, I decided to get a head start on my research and conduct a study on the reading practices and attitudes of the child participants in a Vacation Bible School summer program in my hometown church community. My original study focused on how reading is used in the program, especially during the program's one-on-one reading portion. After transcribing interviews, coding and organizing data, the findings were not surprising. The youths' perceptions of their reading and writing abilities largely rested on what feedback they received in school. Throughout the seminar, I found myself thinking and talking more about my positionality as a researcher, participant, and member. The project became less about the reading practices of members in the community and became more about my positionality as a relocated member returning to do research in my hometown community. I found that researchers as participants and members can use their positionality to think critically about the different layers within their communities.

Jeremy: When beginning the project for class, I knew that I was interested in focusing on zines in some way, but my focus was extremely broad because zines and zine cultures boldly engage in intersectional politics, so I was stumbling to find a specific focus. In-class discussions influenced me to approach the project through ethnographic methods, which meant completing the IRB process and deciding who to interview. I decided to broadly ask the question: "Where are the zines?" in order to explore if and where zinesters are still actively crafting zines and engaging in radical activist work. I chose two current young zinesters—one from the POC zine project and one who recently started making her own zine; a zine archivist who runs the Queer Zine Archive Project based in Milwaukee; a former zinester and current visual and comic artist; and an academic who currently studies grrrl zines. The end result took the form of a hybrid zine with creative theorizing to form a genealogy of zine cultures that incorporated my own poetry alongside interview excerpts and queer theory.

Grace: My primary research interests at the beginning of the semester were in the areas of racial segregation and racism in the community of contemporary poetry. Many recent high-profile events, alongside the pandemic lack of visibility of poets of color and of divergent identities, demonstrated how the white institution of contemporary poetry failed to extend its project to consider the racialized and gendered dimensions of the creation of poetry. Why is it important, if not fundamentally necessary, to intersect discussions of race, class, gender, and other identitarian aspects within spaces of art and creative writing? What might such discussions even look like? What happens when theoretical aestheticizations within the academy collide with the practical realities of institutional power imbalances? Who are the parties most affected and how are they pooling their voices together and pushing back? Where do these conversations usually happen? How have such conversations reshaped the kind of poetry being read, written, and disseminated?

Among the impetuses for this project were our class discussions about blurring the line between theory and praxis and between the academic and political. My initial proposal was to collect original and existing interviews with poets whose publications and public lives were intertwined with literary activism. As the semester continued, I became further drawn to the interdisciplinary nature of the seminar. Borrowing from performance theory and affect theory, I gravitated toward constructing a solid theoretical grounding for some of the questions I posed at the beginning of the seminar.

Muriel: At the beginning of the course, I wanted to explore the conversations emerging in light of several recent politically charged moments in literary politics. As a creative writer, I feel a particular stake in this inquiry as I have often felt a lack of centralized dialogue around these issues. Thus, I sought out several writers whose politics are notably central to their creative work to help answer questions about what it means to be a socially and politically involved writer. However, the content of my interviews with them turned out to be different than anticipated. The recurrent concern across all interviews seem to be a desire for these poets to affirm their creative work in poetry as a legitimate form of labor. Although this focus on poetic labor was not the initial inquiry for this project, I have realized that an investigation of what *work* means in artistic production provides an effective entry point into the greater dialogue of what it means to be a socially and politically engaged artist.

Shannon: From the start of my project, I wasn't quite certain how I would contextualize my findings. My initial idea was to conduct interviews with poets from various communities, asking how they thought their work interacted with the larger world. This was done partly in the interest of my own development, as a way for me to think about how other creative writers were moving through different literary/non literary spheres. And, I wanted to make this information available to those similarly contemplating these questions, as well as analyze how poets viewed themselves as agents towards a goal of change.

Initially, I believed a final paper rife with my own thoughts and opinions would be the best format to tackle this endeavor. But, in the seminar, we discussed how speaking for others becomes a trope of academic discourse, a way to elevate your own opinion or worldview above those who are kind enough to participate in research. When I started to think more concretely about a finalized project, nothing seemed quite right in terms of me gathering data and synthesizing that information through specific lenses. These people were complicated, branching out in tangled directions; the "goals" I had anticipated were more multi-faceted than I'd first perceived them to be, which should have come as no surprise, considering my own scattered relation to the poetry world and how I want to exist within it.

And so, what came out was shaped by my time in Community Literacies, through our conversations around positionality and power hierarchies in academia and other institutional settings. I write, as a small tangent to the introduction of my piece, "I don't want to speak for you. I want to listen. I want to engage. I want to learn. I want to create" (Kenny). The collaborative nature of my project, which pulls from the interviews I conducted to create a digital landscape—a mockup of a website with question-framed forums that have these voices interacting—was birthed from the concepts inherent to our class and how we continuously learned to be aware researchers in an intricate world.

Challenging Academic Publication

Grace: I will be presenting an adapted version of my paper at the 2016 Multi-Ethnic Literature of the United States (MELUS) conference, on a panel titled "Reconciling The Ties That Bind: Aesthetic Innovations and Performing Race in Poetry." In an effort to form a discussion panel that is more collaborative than incidental, I will use the research paper produced through this seminar as a foundation for looking at racial performativity, and adapt it for the panel presentation to include textual and contextual analyses of poets such as Bhanu Kapil and Theresa Hak-Kyung Cha. The panel will, collaboratively, offer a mode of critique that centers race and maintains its primacy in poetry beyond the aesthetic categories dictated primarily by a canon that maintains the "universality" of whiteness.

Muriel: I expressed to Dr. Weinstein in the beginning of the course, as well as to my interviewees, that my goal for this project is to participate in the larger discussion of what it means to be a socially and politically engaged writer. This purpose necessitates publication in a public literary forum with a precedent for publishing essays that critique issues within various literary communities. It is important that my writing is not regarded as "new" but rather as an extension of a dialogue that has been going on for a very long time.

While the final product for the seminar was a hybrid personal and critical essay, I am interested in further experimenting with the formal expectations of academic writing through a blend of lyric essay and poetry forms to communicate the richness of my interviewees' voices as well as my own. I find that experimentation with form and genre is especially necessary for this project as it asks questions about power and authority, notions of which become distorted when boundaries between forms and genres are blurred. Experimenting with the form and presentation of this research also requires me to critique what it means to present a collective voice, to articulate experiences and ideas that occur among poets of color. Play with form can perhaps invite a way for a collective voice to exist while also problematizing any tendency towards essentializing these experiences. Hopefully, it will also allow me to explore ways to place myself within this conversation as a poet of color and a researcher.

Shannon: The poets I interviewed for my research discussed the idea of accessibility, of making information and creative work available to a wider audience. I wanted my project to engage in that accessibility, branching out from mere fodder for other researchers to pick at. What emerged was a website mock-up—a place where poets, writers, and inter-textual artists discussed their process, writing as a medium, and the ways they see their work moving in the world. Each section asked certain questions, and the poets whom I interviewed addressed subjects related to these questions. I also included some of the creative work these artists generated, as well as my own work, to connect perceptions of creativity and creative process to the product itself, and to put myself in the conversation as opposed to positioning myself as an elevated arbiter. Theoretical frameworks—snippets from books which deal with these questions—were also sprinkled through certain sections, to show that academic discourse and this type of experimental format don't have to be at odds.

Challenging the role of researcher

Sarah: Because I chose to study an issue that I am personally and professionally committed to as an activist, I was concerned about confirmation bias. During an in-class discussion about the project, the group offered a couple of strategies for addressing this concern. The first was to acknowledge my positionality and include a transparent analysis of it as part of my project. The second suggestion was to compensate for potential confirmation bias by collaborating with other colleagues.

The second option would have been ideal, but was not feasible given the remaining time left in the semester. The first option proved to be a workable solution. Within my own findings, I was also assured that confirmation bias was at least mitigated because the data actually contradicted many of the common assumptions and tropes with which I was familiar.

Alex: My positionality as a participant and member of the community became a larger focus of my project than I had anticipated. During interviews, I was aware of it as a limitation. Since I was in a teacher role, the children might have felt that they had to provide the "right" answer. Although some of the teens had known me for several years, my older age and the fact that they knew I was conducting research could have made them feel like they also had to provide the "right" answer. I was also made aware of my positionality through the manner in which I was introduced to new members. I was framed as a community role model because I had completed college and am attending graduate school, and in passing comments, I was praised for not being a young unwed mother and for continuing to return to volunteer. But in positioning me as a role model, people didn't take into consideration the special circumstances that enabled me to be a high achiever. I had more privilege than the many undocumented members of my community. I possessed a social security number, which allowed me to qualify for in-state tuition and to receive academic scholarships. By celebrating my academic privilege, in fact, people were devaluing the young single mothers in our community who were working towards or had completed bachelor's degrees. Positioning me as the role model was also problematic in that it reinforced the myth that, with a little hard work and determination, all dreams can come true. In fact, I fear that some members of the community do not fully understand that we should be questioning the institutions that make it nearly impossible for more brown youth to attend college. Instead of praising one member who managed to find a way around systemic hurdles, we should be collectively thinking of ways to ensure that all community members can excel.

Kieran: My greatest regret regarding this project is not that I did not finish everything I intended to—I can complete that research later—but that what I did produce ended up looking little different from a standard English seminar paper. I found myself adopting the impersonal, authorial "I" and supposedly objective eye characteristic of much writing in the humanities. This persona possesses opinions, even interests, but does not feel his own emotions worthy of inclusion, though in reality I found researching and writing about euthanasia, the discourse of animal shelters, and the community of workers who inhabit such spaces upsetting and disheartening. I also found myself writing about communities about which I had little firsthand knowledge. Writing about these organizations' websites without speaking to and observing their members is a little like describing the culture of a city by examining a tourism poster. I suppose this is a testament to the difficulty of setting aside habitual scholarly approaches, especially when they are taught and rewarded by most of the academy.

Jeremy: I have been involved with zines and zinefests for a few years, and I was delighted at the opportunity to think about them in an academic space because of their critiques of power and privilege. However, as a researcher, I felt the need to be aware of my own position as a graduate student with a particularly privileged platform and voice as white, cis-gendered, and male-appearing. In previous conversations with zinesters, I was an active participant, but in my research, I wanted to be careful about what I was adding during the interviews because I really wanted to hear different perspectives on zines and zine communities without imposing my own perspective. At the same time, in crafting the zine I produced for my final seminar project, I was able to put my own perspective in dialogue with their interviews, primarily through poetry.

Matthew: The community I worked with was founded by members of the Black Lives Matter (BLM) movement. Its central aim—to end police brutality—is an issue that disproportionately affects people of color. As a straight, white, able-bodied man taking on a leadership role within this community, it was imperative that I recognize my own privileged positionality. One of the issues I struggled with in writing my final project was the extent to which I should focus on that positionality. The experience of trying to write myself into the community with whom I was working was but another reminder of the difficulty and necessity of critically reflecting on one's own position of power and influence. The disparate power dynamic I experienced in working with Justice Together, a newly-established campus activist group, naturally opened up a host of larger ethical dilemmas: What does it mean to simply *recognize* privilege? What is or should be the role of an ally in social justice work? Who is representing whom? Whose voices are lost or silenced to make space for an ally's? Throughout the semester, these were the kinds of questions we wrestled with in the seminar. In fact, questions of power dynamics and positionality regularly came up in our classroom metadiscourse—from classroom etiquette to trigger topics to conversational ethics. The importance of critically examining the researcher's subjectivity remained central to our collective concerns as student-scholars, in and out the classroom.

Challenging the good intentions we have for our research

Muriel: Throughout my research and particularly in the writing phase, I worried that this work could become another piece romanticizing the agonized efforts of writers of color struggling for visibility, agency, and financial stability. How do I talk about struggle without feeding into the public image of the starving artist? How do I nuance my analysis of the struggles of poets of color in contrast to white artists?

In one of my interviews, a poet talks about their particular struggle to achieve stable, salaried employment in literary organizations while also being gender-nonconforming and non-white. They state that employers view their non-normative gender and racial presentations as unprofessional, despite their extensive literary-organizing experiences and qualifications. It was a necessary story to tell and illustrative of the oppressive tactics that queer poets of color have to contend with to exist as an artist at present. Yet the interviewee was careful to remark that their critique was through their eyes only and could be disputed by others in a number of ways. There was simultaneous critique and care in the way they chose to discuss their circumstances. As a researcher, I wanted to represent this nuance in my writing. I did not want to stop at articulating the idea that oppressive biases exist in literary employment but to show how queer writers of color feel a constant need to verify these moments with others, to second-guess their own interpretations of experiences that *feel* oppressive, and to exercise extreme care when naming violations for fear of losing credibility in the larger literary community.

Conclusion
Challenging English, or, What does it mean for community literacy studies to travel out from Composition and Rhetoric?

Alex: Despite being from different fields, we were all drawn to this seminar on community literacies, which focused on making research not only ethical, but also human. Many times during seminar, I felt grateful to be surrounded by scholars who were willing to step out of their comfort zones and go into the field, meet new people, and then be candid with the group about our projects' challenges. The seminar focused on the processes of our projects, not just the end products, which are what we often obsess about in academia. It also reminded us that research is not just about data and figures. Knowledge stems from experiences, and qualitative researchers have to be careful how we listen to and what we do with people's experiences. In examining other communities, we also *formed* a community whose members can continue to consult with and reach out to one another.

Sarah: Having a seminar focused on community in a large and largely traditional English department meant that many of our discussions centered around making a case for this kind of work, reassuring ourselves that it can be done and is worth doing despite skepticism from colleagues who prefer and privilege more traditional scholarship. It was evident that, as a class, we were all aware of the risks involved in committing to this kind of work. Many of us initially lacked certain vocabulary and knowledge about community literacy work and the various ways it might be executed. There simply aren't many models of or discussions about community literacy or community work in general in a department as traditional as ours. It almost seemed like taking a class outside of the department. The other side of that, though, is that the novelty of a course like this really opened up our creativity, giving us the freedom and incentive to explore new ideas or old ideas that we've never had the opportunity to pursue. And I speak for myself, but I think others might agree, that the distinct character of this seminar among our more traditional English seminars actually helped me fuse disparate aspects of my scholarly identity within and beyond the department.

Kieran: I agree with Alex's and Sarah's comments. As a student of English literature whose partner is a sociology student, I often find myself questioning the social value of the kind of work that is produced by English departments: politically progressive but not activist; concerned with issues of representation but rarely deigning to represent actual communities; and generally written, if not from an armchair, then from a research library. It would not be fair to expect community literacy scholars to reform the traditional English department, but the existence of such a field or methodology or philosophy presents a challenge to the underlying assumptions of how English should be done. On a personal level, although I probably will not change my overall scholarly focus to community literacies or even rhetoric, I have new questions with which to challenge myself when I otherwise might have barged ahead: Why *not* conduct field research? What about non-written forms of discourse? Who am I to write this, and how do I feel about this experience?

Muriel: As a graduate student pursuing my Masters of Fine Arts in creative writing, taking an English seminar that focuses on community literacies has been extremely influential to my writing practice. Alex mentions the importance of research that is not only "ethical, but also human." It is such an interesting note to make, especially since our respective discipline—literature, writing studies, creative writing—are all concerned with "the human," and yet I think there is a simultaneous tendency in academia to flatten the rich diversity of human experiences. What we learned in our seminar is that this flattening tendency stems, in part, from a long history of practices that sought to contain and assert power over marginalized communities—the notion of "good" work masking oppressive practices. If we are not mindful of this history, we can become complicit in these oppressive practices.

Oftentimes, I am told that literature and creative writing have no stakes, that literary merit is based purely on individual genius. I am happy that this course has given me tools to trouble this notion and to approach my own art production and social and political involvement in literary spaces with the understanding that both my work and these spaces are always ideologically inflected. This includes my own current MFA program and English department, which are spaces that allow me to examine community literacies while also belonging to a long tradition of exclusionary academic practices. I'm wary of the ivory tower and what it does with our research on marginalized communities, particularly if we, the researchers, also identify as members of those marginalized communities. This course has made me think about my relationship to my work within the department, to feel and sometimes fight for a sense of ownership over my work, and to constantly interrogate the ways in which I can do this work without compromising my connection to the communities of which I am a part.

Sue: This article began by asking what it means for community literacy studies to be taken up as a category of English studies beyond composition and rhetoric. What we find in the reflections from the LSU seminar participants resonates with a central insight from Bowen et al. Even in a writing studies-specific program, they found that "the incentive to recognize rhetoric and literacy as situated, public, social, and political domains of activity is at odds with the persistent belief that academic success requires a focus on activities removed from civic life" (18). If this is true within writing studies, it is much more so in areas of English studies that have rarely centered social engagement: literature, creative writing, and traditional rhetoric. Yet the reflections in the present article strongly suggest that writing studies and related fields are not the only areas of English in which graduate students find value in purposeful, reflective engagement with communities and literacies beyond the academy.

The work we undertook together in the Researching Community Literacies seminar caused participants to challenge ourselves and one another in sometimes profound ways. As Matthew mentioned in the "Challenging the role of researcher" section above, we had moments of joy and moments of tension; I suspect that some of that tension rose to the surface exactly *because* we were talking so directly about ethical human interaction and situated daily experience. It is, or ought to be, impossible to delve into community literacy studies without ending up remembering one's own experiences and motivations and blind spots. That's challenging stuff anywhere, but added to the pressures and anxieties of graduate study in general, and engagement with mostly unfamiliar, non-academic sites of practice in particular, it generates a special intensity.

The student reflections throughout this article tell a story of intelligent, creative scholars challenging ourselves and one another, asking questions we are not used to asking in academic spaces, connecting with unfamiliar—sometimes uncomfortable—spaces and subjects of study, acknowledging difficulties and disappointments, and emphasizing a humane approach to our academic and creative work. That humaneness is an orientation that surely has more than a linguistic root in common with the humanities; I would suggest that it is, in fact, the great value that community literacy studies can contribute to an English department, whatever its disciplinary makeup.

Works Cited

Bowen, L., K. Arko, J. Beatty, C. Delaney, I. Dorpenyo, L. Moeller, E. Roberts, and J. Velat. "Community Engagement in a Graduate-Level Community Literacy Course." *Community Literacy Journal* 9.1 (2014): 18-38. Web. 29 December 2015.

Fero, Michele, Jim Ridolfo, Jill McKay Chrobak, Deborah Vriend Van Duinen, Jason Wirtz, Ellen Cushman, and Jeffrey T. Grabill. "A Reflection on Teaching and Learning in a Community Literacies Graduate Course." *Community Literacy Journal* 1.2 (2006): 81–93. Web. 29 December 2015

Gee, James Paul. *Social Linguistics and Literacies: Ideology in Discourse*. 2nd ed. New York: Routledge, 1996. Print.

Goffman, Erving. *The Presentation of Self in Everyday Life*. 1st ed. New York: Bantam Doubleday Dell Publishing, 1959. Print.

Higgins, Lorraine, Eleanor Long, and Linda Flower. "Community Literacy: A Rhetorical Model For Personal And Public Inquiry." *Community Literacy Journal* 1.1 (2006): 9-43. Web. 29 December 2015.

Kenny, Shannon. *Unpublished Seminar Paper*. (2016), Louisiana State University.

Long, Elenore. *Community Literacy And The Rhetoric Of Local Publics*. West Lafayette: Parlor Press, 2008. Print.

Paris, Django and Maisha T. Winn, eds. *Humanizing Research: Decolonizing Qualitative Inquiry with Youth and Communities*. Thousand Oaks: SAGE Publications, 2013. Print.

Pezzullo, Phaedra C. "Resisting 'National Breast Cancer Awareness Month: The rhetoric of counterpublics and their cultural performances." *Quarterly Journal of Speech* 89:4 (2003): 345-365. Web. 29 December 2015.

_____. "Touring 'Cancer Alley,' Louisiana: Performances of Community and Memory for Environmental Justice." *Text and Performance Quarterly* 23:3 (2010): 226-252. Web. 29 December 2015.

Street, Brian V. *Literacy in Theory and Practice*. Cambridge: Cambridge University Press, 1985. Print.

Author Bios

Sue Weinstein is an associate professor of English at Louisiana State University, teaching English secondary education, language development and diversity, literacy studies, and poetry. She is currently completing a book (tentatively) titled *The Room Is on Fire: An Overview of the International Youth Spoken Word Poetry Movement*. Her first book, *Feel These Words: Writing in the Lives of Urban Youth*, was published by SUNY Press in 2009. Before entering graduate school, Sue taught high school English Language Arts in Chicago, Illinois and Cochabamba, Bolivia. Her review of New Orleans' Neighborhood Story Project books appeared in the first issue of *Community Literacy Journal*.

Jeremy Cornelius is an English PhD student at Louisiana State University. He currently works in queer theory, visual studies, southern studies, and digital humanities with a focus on comics, zines, and visual poetry. Before enrolling at LSU, he worked as the Program Assistant for the Sexualities Project at Northwestern and handled social media for ArtWell in Philadelphia. He will be researching zines in the residency program at the Queer Zine Archive Project in Milwaukee this summer.

Shannon Kenny is an MFA candidate in creative writing at Louisiana State University. She does performance work at the Eclectic Truth Poetry Slam and Open Mic in downtown Baton Rouge, competing in events such as the Woman's Poetry Slam and Grand Slam Finals. Prior to attending LSU, Shannon was involved in archaeology projects centered around community outreach on the Island of Inishbofin and Dunluce Castle in Northern Ireland. Currently, Shannon writes on disability justice as well as visual/sonic poetics.

Muriel Leung is an MFA candidate in creative writing at Louisiana State University. Prior to her graduate study, she managed and taught multi-disciplinary arts programming to youth and older adults with a focus on social justice activism throughout New York City with such organizations as Community-Word Project, Elders Share the Arts, Sadie Nash Leadership Project, and others. Her first poetry collection, *Bone Confetti*, is forthcoming from Noemi Press in October 2016.

Grace Shuyi Liew's poetry chapbooks *Prop* (Ahsahta Press) and *Book of Interludes* (Anomalous Press) are forthcoming in 2016, and her poetry, essays, and reviews can be found online and in print. Her work intersects with postcolonial feminism, queer theory, transnational migrations, and critical race theories. She is from Malaysia and currently she teaches women and gender studies at LSU, where she is also earning her MFA. Through a residency with the Manship Theatre at the Shaw Center for the Arts, she is also a teaching artist who works in K-12 schools.

Kieran Lyons is a PhD student in English literature at Louisiana State University, where he also teaches writing. He received an M.F.A. in fiction writing from the University of Mississippi and a B.A. in cognitive sciences and studio art from Rice University. He is interested in interdisciplinary approaches to studying animals, food, and global literatures.

Matthew Tougas is a second-year PhD student in English (Writing and Culture) at LSU where, in addition to teaching first- and second-year composition courses, he serves as the director of *Justice Together at LSU* and is a founding member of LSU's *Rhetoric Society of America* chapter. Matthew earned his bachelor's degree at the University of Kansas and his master's at the University of New Mexico, both with concentrations in Rhetoric and Composition. Currently, he is a member of the Writing Program Administrators-Graduate Organization's (WPA-GO) Graduate Committee.

Alejandra Torres is an English PhD student and Women's and Gender Studies minor at Louisiana State University. Her main research interests include literacy, culture, and age studies. She is interested in the role affect plays in educational settings and how literature and writing can allow students to reflect upon their own development.

Sarah L. Webb is a PhD student in the Department of English at Louisiana State University. Her primary research interests include literacy, digital media, and black women's studies. Before enrolling at LSU, she managed websites and social media accounts for local TV stations, taught high school English and college writing courses, and worked as a freelance writer and editor. For many years Sarah has engaged in youth mentoring and community work. She also maintains a blog, ColorismHealing.org, through which she hosts writing contests and other literacy events.

Interview with Steve Parks

Jennifer Hitchcock

Abstract

Jennifer Hitchcock interviews community activist and director of Syracuse University's Composition and Cultural Rhetoric doctoral program, Steve Parks. They discuss Parks's working-class background, career path, influences, and activism. Parks also considers the direction of the field of composition and rhetoric and expresses optimism for the future.

Introduction

Steve Parks is an accomplished composition and rhetoric scholar, teacher, and community activist, and he currently serves as the director of Syracuse University's Composition and Cultural Rhetoric doctoral program. He received his doctorate from the University of Pittsburgh in 1994 with a dissertation focused on the history of the 1974 CCCCs' "Students' Right to Their Own Language" statement, a revised version of which was published in book form as *Class Politics: The Movement for "The Students' Right to Their Own Language"* as part of NCTE's Refiguring English Studies series.

While an assistant professor at Temple University from 1997 to 2004, Parks directed New City Writing: A Research Institute for the Study and Practice of Literature, Literacy, and Culture, and he founded New City Community Press (NCCP) in 1998. NCCP publishes a variety of community literacy collections about urban life, local culture, economic rights, and social justice, giving local communities the opportunity to tell their own stories and have their voices address important national and global issues. Among its other work, NCCP also publishes the peer-reviewed academic journal, *Reflections: A Journal of Public Rhetoric, Civic Writing, and Service Learning*, for which Parks has also served as an editor.

In recent years, much of Parks's scholarship has focused on how writing and the field of composition and rhetoric can promote social change and grassroots activism. Parks and Eli Goldblatt discuss the ways that WAC programs can serve as productive locations for writing programs to connect with local communities in "Writing

Beyond the Curriculum." The idea of "writing beyond the curriculum" is further explored in his 2010 book, *Gravyland: Writing Beyond the Curriculum in the City of Brotherly Love*. In "Sinners Welcome: The Limits of Rhetorical Agency," he draws on Cornel West's concept of "prophetic pragmatism" and Parks' own experiences with a community publishing project to argue that the field must move beyond mere discussion of progressive social values and a focus on the rhetorical agency of marginalized groups to instead do more to actually participate in collective action and real political organizing. And in "Strategic Speculations on the Question of Value: The Role of Community Publishing in English Studies," Parks examines a problematic community publishing project and argues that the "use-value" of texts must be more of a focus in the field. Through discussion of a successful international student and community writing collective in "Emergent Strategies for an Established Field: The Role of Worker Writer Collectives in Composition and Rhetoric," Parks argues for replacing the "contact zone" with more community-based collectives or "federations."

Throughout most of his career, Parks's scholarship and teaching have been directly connected to activist and public rhetorics through community publishing and grassroots, collective action. While the field of composition and rhetoric has long been concerned with progressive values and educating students for democratic citizenship, Parks couples these values with on-the-ground action and a concern for the success of working-class students in the academy.

Interview

JH: What led you to advocate for a greater focus on collective action for political and social change initially? Was it your work with New City Community Press and community partnerships like the one you describe in "Sinners Welcome" and *Gravyland*? Or did you begin to see the importance of collective action even earlier—maybe during your graduate study at the University of Pittsburgh, as you discuss in the introduction to *Gravyland*? How did you come to believe in the importance of collective action?

SP: I began to study composition and rhetoric right when the field was pivoting between two different historical moments. One the one hand, you had the 1960s and '70s, which were marked by a sense of the academic, the composition teacher, as an advocate and activist, both for students and for institutional/political change. On the other, you had in the late '70s and heading into the '80s, a real push to become a discipline, to model yourself after versions of English departments. Here scholarship was the coin of the realm, not efforts to create systemic change for working-class students entering the academy. I can remember being in graduate school in the '80s and experiencing that shift, noticing who I was teaching at Pitt, who was entering our graduate program compared to previous cohorts of graduate students. And this was all happening in the context of the economy in Pittsburgh shattering. A lot of my friends' fathers and parents lost their jobs. Whole communities were wiped out as the steel industry collapsed. I can remember admiring the steel workers and community activists who were trying, somewhat futilely, to get the steel mills to stay, but also demand that the steel mills do right by the community on their way out. And I remember admiring the communities who organized to support their children to go to college.

It struck me odd, wrong really, that the field was turning toward a more disciplinary identity when the tradition that would be most useful to the working class students in my classrooms harkened back more to the '60s and '70s. So it was that experience of entering the field at a moment when it was leaving its activist roots that led me to think, "Well, what is my responsibility as somebody who, through the support of the community, managed to go to college? What's my responsibility to the people who didn't have the opportunity?" And that led me to think of activism as it was characterized in the '60s by Geneva Smitherman, Richard Ohmann, and folks like that. That's what led me to that set of issues.

How do you see your current work fitting into the history of the field of composition and rhetoric? What figures and movements in the field have most influenced you? You mentioned Smitherman and what was going on at the time in the '60s and '70s, and you also cite Linda Flower in some of your work. But who and what else in comp/rhet have influenced you the most?

It's interesting because I believe I was at the last CCCCs that Kenneth Burke attended. Anne Berthoff was there and so was Peter Elbow—the whole set of folks who in some way were the historical predecessors to my time in the field. I was also fortunate enough to know Jim Berlin. And I studied with Bartholomae. I have been like the Forrest Gump of composition. I have always managed to know the people who played a significant part in defining the work of the field.

To a great extent, however, very few of them actually influenced my own work. In fact, for a long time, I used to let people know that I have only ever taken one composition/rhetoric course. It was a course with Bartholomae on the history of composition. I never took a basic writing seminar. I never took a WPA seminar. Never took a classical rhetoric seminar. So I don't necessarily point back to that scholarship or those individuals as having influenced me. The people who influenced my sense of what I wanted to be as a professional were people who were the activists of the '60s. So, Al Haber, who nobody writes about in composition, fascinated me because as he left graduate school and became part of the academy, he helped form the New University Conference (NUC). The NUC was this interdisciplinary group of graduate students and faculty who were committed to linking their work to community and social change. I see my work as emerging much more out of that activist context than any particular composition/rhetoric scholar.

I was also in graduate school when cultural studies was dominant. So as I looked for modern theories of politics, activism, and social change, I looked to Derrida, Foucault, Spivak, to poststructuralist readings of Marx. These texts gave me a sense of how power operates, what ideology is, what agency means, what collective agency looks like in practice. They gave me a certain political definition of the university that, when coupled with a sense of 60's activism, helped me define what I took to be the work of the first-year writing class. Then, only really as a third stage in the process, did I begin to look for people in composition and rhetoric. At that point, Berlin was important to me, in part because *Rhetoric and Reality* had that social-epistemic argument which related to discussions of class and discussions of ideology. He also interested me because he was in the Marxist Literary group, which is how I met him. And once again, it was an interdisciplinary group that looked at how Marx could be used in the academy and outside of it. Geneva Smitherman intrigued me in part because of her scholarship, but also because she was active in the Black Caucus, and I was interested in how people in the field were organizing politically. So I looked to folks like Karen Hollis and Ira Shor because I found an affinity with them because of their work in the Progressive Caucus and their dual focus on working-class pedagogy and politics.

So, in a sense, the way in which I encountered scholars in composition and rhetoric was through their activism and then I read their scholarship in light of that larger activist paradigm, connected it to things that I was interested in, and began to invoke them in my writing as a way to try to bring in some of the issues I thought were important. I should add that I was also writing at a time when a lot of the scholarship was student-paper driven, mainly around cognitive studies, error studies; Linda Flower was still doing social-cognitive rhetoric. I wasn't aware of a lot of people writing about politics or agency or students as political beings, so I felt there was no one for me to draw upon, except Ira Shor maybe, who was doing that writing, so I felt had to go other places.

Related to that, I wanted to ask if there any other figures in the field that you think have a lot to offer in the area of public or civic rhetoric? Anyone that you didn't already mention?

The field tends to create hero narratives: "Then there was Dave Bartholomae. Then there was Linda Flower." I get that, and I admire their work. Still, I would say that the people who were doing civically minded and politically oriented activism that interested me were people who the field has somewhat forgotten about: Louis Crew, who was one of the first "out" gay scholars and certainly one of the first folks to bring those issues into the field. I don't think his work is ever really cited, but I think he was a pivotal figure. He edited the first *College English* around sexuality. Carlotta Dwyer, who helped form the Latino Caucus, did a lot of work in developing the idea of a Latino writer in our field. She used to go around and listen to street poets and handwrite their poetry in order to begin to record it. I'm not sure she is adequately represented in the history of our field. Richard Ohmann is in some ways a huge figure, but in some ways is no longer cited, which has to do with us thinking that "class" is a dead category—an opinion I clearly don't think is true.

I think people who had an idea that crossed disciplines, crossed boundaries, and imagined that intervening in the field took building a new collective identity and a new collective sense of who our students were and what our responsibilities were to them were pivotal to the field's development. Here I'm thinking about many of the members of *CCCCs'* caucuses and special interest groups, but that probably also didn't publish that much. Maybe they published textbooks, but they didn't publish the *CCCCs'* article; they didn't do the university press book. They probably taught four/four. Worked for justice in their immediate contexts. And as our field moved in the '80s to thinking of itself as a traditional discipline, their work didn't have the public context to be cited. So they fell off the map. But for people who, prior to when you had doctorates and MAs in rhet/comp, were busy inventing what it meant to teach writing in the '70s and early '80s, they know who these people are. It's a shame that the whole field doesn't.

I hadn't thought about that. I have read a lot of alternative histories of the field in Louise Phelps's class in my PhD program at ODU. But obviously where they publish is going to be a huge factor in how they are remembered.

A lot of alternative histories tend to focus on alternative sites of teaching. They don't go back and try to reclaim figures who were at that borderline when we were political and pre-disciplinary. The work that those folks did, that scene has been lost. And in the process we have forgotten that there were alternative ways to imagine our professional identity.

One of the figures we read, Jim Zebroski, was somebody who brought up lots of issues related to class. His work stood out to me as being really interesting and focused on different elements that a lot of the other histories leave out. And then there was work by Keith Gilyard and Jacqueline Jones Royster and others who were pulling out figures from the past who have been overlooked for one reason or another.

I remember when I was in grad school, when I took my only comp/rhet course with Bartholomae. He said, "You know, none of the people we are reading in class have Composition and Rhetoric degrees." They had literature degrees, psychology degrees, linguistics degrees. His point was that this notion of a specific degree was a recent historical phenomenon, and a lot of the people who drew upon multiple disciplinary interests are less interesting to the field now as the field decides that it's producing its own knowledge and doesn't have to draw off other disciplines as much.

So "writing about writing" is in effect arguing that comp/rhet doesn't need to pull off of other disciplines because we now know what writing is. It is like a culminating consolidation moment that has been happening since the '80s. And I think it is that consolidation into a field that has left behind many important figures, left behind a whole different way of acting as a professional.

Service learning was seen as "civic," and that turned into "community partnership," which was "civic" plus a little agitation. But if you go back and look at Geneva Smitherman, she was doing hardcore organizing. These folks were thinking of the discipline and conferences as a place to learn organizing tactics to take back to where they taught because they recognized that for the student to be in the classroom the whole system has to change. And that's been lost, I think. Maybe it's coming back a bit though. Linda Adler-Kassner's *The Activist WPA* draws off Marshall Ganz who does community organizing based on his work with SNCC and Caesar Chavez, and so she is reanimating it in a way. She is not invoking the New University Conference, or Progressive Caucus, or the Black Caucus, but she is drawing on that history to say we have to do more if we want diverse students from all backgrounds in our classrooms.

When you describe what you do within composition and rhetoric, what terms do you prefer? "Activist rhetoric," "public rhetoric," "civic rhetoric," etc.? Which terms do you end up using about your own work, and why?

That's tricky. One of the people I studied with in graduate school at the University of Pittsburgh was Gayatri Spivak, probably the most significant teacher I ever had in my life. I can remember chatting with her once. She was saying that she was going to give a talk at a conference in India based on subaltern rhetorics and was going to wear a professional business suit because "wherever I am, I like to surprise and change the context a bit." Everybody was expecting "X," so she decided she would format her identity slightly differently. And I remember thinking that the lesson there was that whatever label you take on, you have to be very tactical about it.

So I probably have used all of those terms at different points, but it has always been context-specific. If I am arguing to the Dean that I want funding to take working-class students to London to do writing with working-class writers as part of an attempt to write a working-class manifesto, then I will call it "service learning." If I am working on Linda Flower's work, which I admire, but I am trying to make the point that the field has settled for a weak sense of agency, I might position myself as doing "community partnership" work and try to push community partnership work beyond where it currently is because Linda Flower uses "community literacy" as her term.

So I am less concerned about the term that I am identified with than how I can use the term to push the debate in a certain way, which kind of goes back to the fact that I had this introduction to the field that wasn't based upon reading a lot of composition/

rhetoric scholarship. I came into the field with a set of allegiances and thoughts about what the field stood for politically. I am interested in what term you can deploy at that moment that is going to push that politics along. I have been a "partnership" person. I have been a "community literacy" person, I have been a "civic engagement" person. I have done "service learning." But, at heart, I am always trying to be a progressive scholar, a socially committed person. So it is always a question, to me, of what term at what moment will push that agenda along.

That makes sense. It is very rhetorical of you.

That's what Spivak was teaching me. You need to be rhetorical about your identity. Don't essentialize it. Think of how you are trying to intervene in everything you do.

In "Writing Beyond the Curriculum" and in your book, *Gravyland*, you discuss how to foster engagement with the community outside of the classroom. Do you think interested individual composition instructors should pursue community partnerships, such as service learning projects? Or do you think institutional support or being part of a wider network or "interdisciplinary counter institutional space" or "counterspace," as you discuss, are necessities for such work?

There is a big grandiose answer to that. I would say for faculty who are not in the tenure stream, who are adjuncting at a pitiful pay rate and little security, I think service learning isn't the best use of their time. I think their extra hours should be devoted to working to unionize or to support their union to solidify their economic position. I think for graduate students it is important from the moment they begin their career to think about how they are going to relate to the neighborhoods that surround the university they'll eventually work in. But you have to have a real theory of community change and agency, and you really have to know the community you are going into. So I have tended to tell graduate students it should be a pivotal part of your education, and you should construct classes—and I have had some fantastic students who have done amazing things—but you really should wait a year or two and really learn the community before undertaking such work in your graduate career.

And I think the role of individual faculty is to become deeply enmeshed in the community in which you live and listen patiently for a while and eventually see which community invites you in to be part of their collective struggle, and then to think through how the limited skills of the academy can relate to larger systemic issues. I think individual faculty can model an ethical practice, and part of that ethical practice is drawing the resources out of the university and into those community collective struggles. Then, as you model that, it is important for faculty to join together.

At Temple University, I had an institute, created with my close colleague Eli Goldblatt. My goal with the institute was to try to move from that individual tactical intervention and to create a strategic space in the university to support community activism. My sense was that the one thing universities can do well is generate money and spend it. And the one thing that resource-poor communities have a hard time doing—and this very true of non-profits—is generating money and having the ability to spend it. Strategically, if you can get faculty to develop enough ethical partnerships to create an institute, you can then use that location to help fund the collective struggles of the communities around you. And I think in doing so, you can create a node within an otherwise neo-liberal corporate university that can affect a different practice. If you can do that well, you can model to graduate students and undergraduate students what it means to take your knowledge and put it into the service of something greater than a journal or a grade. So it is within that framework that I would think about how service learning or activism operates.

Regarding the idea of the "counterspace," it is possible to create alliances with your colleagues and community members to have a discursive and material space where different types of work can be done. One of the legacies that I admire about organizations like the Black Caucus is that it has created a space that has been sustained for decades, that has generated partnership work, scholarship work. The caucus has mentored students into the field in a way that pushes against the field's limitations. When our principle models are the celebrity scholars, we forget about these different collective traditions. So the counter-institutional space was a way of saying there is a way to act collectively that you'll find much more sustaining in the long term. Dave Bartholomae said this hilarious thing once that someone reported to me. He said, "You know, I'm really famous until I step outside the conference." I think what he was saying was we mistake disciplinary status for actual importance. The counterspace was a way to think through what it would mean to be important.

Outside of your role as a scholar and teacher, do you participate in any activist work that is completely separate from your other scholarship and teaching in the field? And if so, do you see that work as relating to your scholarship and teaching indirectly?

That is sort of a "yes/no" answer. When I was in grad school and I had two kids and no money, very limited health insurance, and no childcare, I was very active in organizing for student benefits. When I was at Temple, there was a whole set of immigrant rights and housing rights, etc. to work on. Since I have been at Syracuse, I have been active in the anti-gentrification struggle in the near West Side, though not nearly involved as my graduate student Ben Kuebrich, who has done great work there.

At all of these moments, though, I have always also been located in the university. Since I was a young adult, I have either taught at the university as a grad student or worked there full-time. And I have always thought it seemed somewhat odd that if I am in such a filthy rich institution, which a lot of colleges are compared to the neighborhood that surrounds them, that I wouldn't try to get those dollars out into the projects that I am working for. So I have consciously never drawn a distinct line between the two because if you are in the near West Side and this community group has nobody who can go door-to-door and find out what the community thinks about police cameras coming in, for instance, and I have a class where students are learning the rhetoric of activism, it seems wrong for me to hold them apart. It limits the students' education and keeps resources that could benefit the community. So, no, I don't have anything I have done in a community that I don't consciously try to integrate into everything else that I do. I don't understand why people do that, but that might also be a personality thing. That might really be my inability to hold things separate, so I would not hold myself up as a model.

It makes sense when one's career takes up so much time and effort, that if you can integrate your activism into that rather than add it on totally separately, it might work out more efficiently.

I can remember when my wife and I were in grad school and we were starting our careers, all the professors at conferences were always saying, "I am so busy. I am so busy. I am way behind on this article." We can remember thinking at that time, all you're really doing is writing an article. You're not digging a ditch, you're not serving burgers, you are not being told to work 70 hours a week like my parents and friends. Of course, I'm older now and can understand the tension a bit better—articles help you get tenure, which help you with economic security; some articles can intervene and change the field. Most folks aren't just writing articles, they are running programs, caring for families. Still, just thinking about my own situation, I think if my very limited work schedule does not allow me to go to a community meeting then I must be lousy at time management. As a full-time Research I tenured professor, I usually teach six hours a week. Given that luxury, it seems disingenuous to say I can't manage my time to do something more than teach.

I also don't expect any sympathy for being behind on an article because I have so much of my own time that I can control. I think I should be able to do more than that. I just should. It seems to me that our discipline has so heightened this scholarly profile that we have decided that's enough and we manage our time badly. For me, I think this rhetoric about being too busy is sometimes an alibi for my lack of time management skills more than anything else. If you are in grad school with kids, then you are screwed and are just trying to survive. I have a student now who has to work at a restaurant full-time because his stipend doesn't pay him enough to support his family, so I get that. But the filthy rich paid professor teaching 1-1 like myself? No. No excuses.

It helps to keep in perspective what a lot of other people, especially working-class people in the community, have to do to get by.

My dad fixed radars on tugboats sixty hours a week, and I made more summer teaching than he made all year. So what, am I going to complain about that? How ridiculous would that be?

In "Sinners Welcome" and some of your other scholarship, you stress the importance of agency—as you were saying, to go beyond "rhetorical agency." Could you go more into how you view agency and how some parts of the field may have a limited idea about agency?

The thing about "Sinners Welcome" is I am afraid it comes off a little too harshly on Linda Flower. She's fantastic. She has done amazing things. I was using the fact that everybody loves Linda Flower's work to question why we would accept a model where we teach people to talk politely to political leaders as our only view of agency, when we know talking politely to political leaders—unless you have a thousand people behind you—isn't going to produce anything. I was interested in that broad-based acceptance, so that's why I wrote that article. That idea of agency, of polite talk and civic discourse, is a nice way to make what we do seemingly culturally important. And it's a way to claim that arguments can change power because we are good at teaching argument. But most people who have changed power that I have read, like Martin Luther King or Caesar Chavez, have always linked their arguments up to broad-scale systemic mass movements. This is what Nancy Welsh's work is about: Yes, we do need to teach people to be rhetorically savvy, but part of that education should also be about getting a bunch of people to be part of your movement.

I think that as we have become a discipline and we have increasingly worried about our status—"are we respected as much as English?"—we have taken on an argument that is appealing to the university but ineffective for our students. That's what I was trying to say. The definition of agency that created our field and put working-class students in our classrooms is not the agency that we are teaching our students to use now, and it is not the agency we are invoking in our scholarship. And in that way, we are leaving behind all of the people we claim to care about in our scholarship. So I thought that wasn't right; that's just ethically wrong.

I studied postmodernism where you are supposed to think nothing is "right" and nothing is "wrong" in an essentialist sense, and, yeah, I believe that. But I also have read Amartya Sen where he says there are fundamental human rights. One of them should be that everyone has access to an education that will empower them to create the society in which they want to live. And we have left that definition behind in our work. We have said it is enough to teach people how to be persuasive in front of people with power who could care less about what most working poor people have to say. And I just refuse to think that that's where our discipline is headed and that it's going to accept that definition.

I think this generation of grad students who are carrying more debt than any previous generation, who have voted for or against the first African American president, who have experienced the recession, who have seen two wars, I can't believe that this generation will be satisfied with the definition of agency which is strictly limited to the politics of manners. They have just experienced too much systemic violence to think that is an adequate solution to the moment. So when I think about my grad students or the grad students I talk to at conferences, I think the next generation is going to fulfill a lot of the promises that folks like myself and Adler-Kassner and Victor Villanueva and others have been hoping for. I think we are about to flip back to a more engaged period in the field.

The description of the failure of the Glassville project in "Strategic Speculations on the Question of Value" reminded me of some of Paula Mathieu's discussion of failed service learning projects from her book, *Tactics of Hope*, which I read when I was studying under Diana George at Virginia Tech.

She's the best. I love Diana George. I think Diana George is a great model of an academic activist. My goal is to be Diana George.

Diana is great. She has definitely also inspired me a lot too. So you have also argued in some of your work that tactics aren't enough and we should focus more on collective action that can lead to real social change. For example, in "Emergent Strategies," you say, "to invoke the language of de Certeau, it became clear that the TAWFF project had become a tactic (a small intervention working off what the system will allow), but not a strategy (the establishment on a solid space from which to enact systemic change)." Could you say a little about how you view the relationship between tactics and a larger strategy for collective action? Depending on the political or institutional location, what if there is not yet a "solid space" in which to establish a larger strategy? Is it ever appropriate to concentrate on short-term tactics in the absence of an effective long-term strategy—or must a well-developed long-term strategy always come first? What if the long-term strategy or even the end goal is undecided or in dispute?

Okay, there's a lot there. There are a couple of responses. On the one hand, of course, in certain contexts, in the immediate moment, the best you can do is to try to throw a wrench into the assembly line. This moment when at the very least I am going to stop this thing from happening.

It reminds me of the Mario Savio quote from the Berkeley Free Speech Movement.

To throw yourself into the machine. So, of course, sometimes the tactic is "the system is screwed, but I will not let this student fall victim to it." It's completely ethical. You have to act in whatever ways it is possible for you to act. But I think within those individualized tactical moments, there is also an underlying ethical set of commitments and an implicit sense of strategy of what it would mean to change the system. So it wouldn't just be a tactic. It could also simultaneously be about creating a policy; it could be about a structure. Any individual moment works within a larger paradigm. And the reason that things stay at the tactical level so much with faculty in the academy is that we don't do a lot of training in graduate education on how you build community, how you build a movement, how you understand that you share common values and then chart out a course that will enact those values. So consequently, I think grad students are taught to think just at the level of tactics. But if you were to make part of graduate education about this sense of how one would move from step one to step two to step three, I think you would find on a value level that a lot of faculty would share common agreement and could, in fact, plan for strategic spaces.

I do tactical stuff all the time; it's not like I am always grandiose-big-strategy-space guy. I have been fortunate enough to work with organizers who have taught me how to move from tactic to strategy, and I have seen the power of when your tactical moment becomes a policy for those to whom you are most indebted and want to help and work with—that I always think you should point towards that.

And I hope that Mathieu would agree with this. I think Mathieu herself would say that she has been cartooned into thinking just tactics when she has a more nuanced view. But for faculty to say tactics are enough is to say, "Well, my privilege is set. I'm okay, so my marginal tactical thing for you will stand for my political commitment." I think the people we work with deserve better than that. Spivak used to say all the time, you have to learn "your privilege is your loss," meaning you have to realize you live in this bubble, and you don't necessarily understand how the world operates, and so what you think is important is minor or trivial to most people. Tactics are important in the bubble of limited activism in the academy. But the working poor and the oppressed and those who live on the wrong side of privilege, they need strategic change. So I think you have to leave your privilege bubble and think hard about what it would mean to be part of that generalized strategy.

I just have one last question. You have discussed scholarship, teaching, and activism as entwined, and you suggest that as scholars and teachers we have an obligation to actively work to be part of the solution to social problems that our field often discusses. Do you see any limitations to scholarship in action—both in terms of

constraints on it from structures, conditions, and realities about how institutions and communities work and in terms of your own sense of what our position can't explain or address?

Scholarship in action was the term that my chancellor used at Syracuse University. In that context, it began as an effort to help faculty take on social justice campaigns, which she put a lot of money towards, but through the years it turned into more neo-liberal gentrification projects. I think that is because the institution is stronger than any particular individual's willpower. What I would say about this is that the real limitation on activism in our field is the beggaring and poverty that the field has placed upon the majority of our teachers. Realistically, if you are teaching four/four/four, and you are a part-time teacher, which is at least 70% of our field, the chances of your classroom being an activist site are small. The labor conditions just beat you down. That isn't to say that there aren't teachers in this situation that haven't done incredible things, but I think systemically, it is very hard to do. In that way, maybe some of the best activism our field could take right now is around labor rights. Change the status of our teachers and you change their ability to take on some of the promises we have made to the larger culture. I think the biggest limitation on our field living up to our promises is the economic condition of our field.

The second limitation is the way in which assessment is operating—in public schools and in state legislatures—it is changing how students are being taught to write in high school and the writing they are expected to produce in college. But all those structures impinge upon our ability to move our classrooms into civic culture in a way that a lot of folks would like.

The other thing is—to be brutally honest about my own status—I think the field and Research I scholars who publish and people in privileged positions have the great fortune to claim that our field should be activist. But I think the majority of the field looks at their working-class students and thinks the most activist thing they could do is to get them to pass Writing 101. I think that is deeply honorable work, and I think that's a progressive thing to do, but that's the activism of our field. When I taught at Temple, I was always proudest of the fact that my first-generation students passed my class and went on to be successful. I don't know. That is the activism going on that we don't talk about as much anymore. I think sometimes Research I scholars who are in such privileged positions can claim a larger vision and miss the deep work that other people are doing.

I am deeply, deeply aware of my own limitations and lack of success in activism. That's why I write about things that don't work because I have an idea that I have been trying to figure out, and I have never quite gotten there. I often just feel really humble when I talk to really great activists. I think, "I wish I could do more than write an article." That's how I feel about activism. There are so many people out there to admire, and I think maybe one day I will be like them. There's so many people I could name, people I meet on the street. I admire Mark Lyons, who does immigrant work in Philly, stands in front of the police as they try to arrest people and take them to the detention center. If I could be like Mark Lyons one day, then, I would say, "There." Then I would have done something, and I would feel proud of myself.

I think you are being humble. You have done a lot. There is a quote from Paula Mathieu in *Tactics of Hope* **about the "radical insufficiency" of all of our acts. I feel like she was talking about how not to get burned out as an activist and how not to feel hopeless because there are so many problems and they are so big, and it is so hard to change them. I think she had a really good discussion about how not to lose hope, which I guess was part of the point of the book.**

I mean this as a compliment, but you could almost turn her book into a quote-a-day calendar, a Mathieu inspiration moment every day. She is a brilliant writer.

Is there anything else you wanted to add about anything?

I began by saying that I didn't enter the field through composition and rhetoric scholarship, and it was very difficult for me to find people that I drew upon for the work that I do. But really, knowing the graduate students I work with now, I have immense hope in this next generation of comp/rhet scholars. They have a much larger proactive vision of what we can be— particularly when I think of the dissertations and the projects and the way they approach the field. It is the greatest thing when you see what is coming. I entered the field through something else and found a way, but I am really excited about what the next generation of folks are about to produce.

Author Bio

Jennifer Hitchcock is a part-time composition instructor and a PhD student in Old Dominion University's English department. Her PhD focus is in Rhetoric, Writing, and Discourse Studies.

Book & New Media Reviews

Saul Hernandez, Intern
Georgia College and State University

Ryan Cresawn, Intern
University of Arizona

From the Book & New Media Review Editor's Desk

Jessica Shumake, University of Arizona

In a recent literacy collaboration with Sunnyside High School students and teachers in Tucson, Arizona, I had the privilege to read and offer feedback on students' scholarship applications and personal statements for college. One student brought her academic transcript to our session because she was hoping she could explain to critical readers the reason for a low grade in one of her classes. I asked her to tell me a little about the class in which she received the low grade so that we could integrate her experience into her personal statement. The story the student shared stopped me cold.

"We got a new teacher that year," she stammered. "The teacher was from Iowa and was much harder than our previous teacher who went on maternity leave." The student continued to explain that most honors classes at her high school were taught very much like the regular sections of any given class. However, the new teacher from Iowa was adamant that honors students needed to have additional challenges, assignments, and homework. The student admitted sheepishly that she "just couldn't meet the teacher's standards and expectations" and barely squeaked by with a D in the course. The student also shared that the teacher left the position after one year, but before resigning told the class that her decision to leave was based on her observation that the students in her classes were not academically prepared to be successful in college and that she would never allow her own child to attend a school in the district. The inappropriate forthrightness on the part of the teacher from Iowa cast a shadow over the student's perception of herself and her readiness for college. A 750-word personal statement is a net whose mesh allows many hardships to slip through in the interest of concision. Fortunately, this issue's keyword essay and review writers are less constrained in their ability to reflect upon educational access and efforts to write one's way out of constrained mindsets and situations.

The overriding theme in Maria Conti's review of David Coogan's *Writing Our Way Out* is the importance of listening to the voices of incarcerated writers as their citizen-selves are produced when they critique "the severely flawed systems that govern their daily lives." Anthony Boynton's review likewise takes a stand for historically marginalized communities to examine how Linda Spears-Bunton and Rebecca Powell's *Toward a Literacy of Promise: Joining the African American Struggle* invites scholars and teachers of the rhetoric of social change to embrace critical literacy as a "humanizing force and a vehicle for political participation and citizenry." Finally, this issue's keyword essay "Place-Based Literacies" by Rosanne Carlo explores recent scholarship in urban and rural literacy studies to highlight how community literacy researchers and practitioners are actively shaping and transforming the social and ecological realities of their neighborhoods and institutions through non-dominant "world-making and world-revealing practices."

Keyword Essay: Place-Based Literacies

Rosanne Carlo
College of Staten Island (CUNY)

Practicing community outreach and research—alongside writing community scholarship—requires an attention to place in the present, as a literal site of practice with material conditions. It also requires an attention to place in the past and future, as an imaginary as well as historical engagement of what a place once was for people and what it has yet to become. Literacy work is, as Paulo Freire describes, a "constant unveiling of reality" (8) toward the end of creating "revolutionary futurity" (10). Explained in more concrete terms, when "people develop their power to perceive critically *the way they exist* in the world and *with which* and *in which* they find themselves" then they can begin to transform their reality, both ecologically and socially (Freire 9). Community work and scholarship continually unveils reality to change and shape it, and this process is a form of place-making.

It is hard to separate the words of education and community scholars from the locations through and in which they write; location is not a backdrop for abstract theories of literacy, but it is the source of those investigations. For example, rural Nebraska and its prairie shapes Robert Brooke's reflections on place-conscious education as a way to create responsive citizens (*Rural Voices: Place-Conscious Education and the Teaching of Writing*); Harlem's crowded streets after a show at the Apollo are the rhythms behind Valerie Kinloch's arguments for a critical stance toward gentrification and loss of black culture (*Harlem on Our Minds: Place, Race, and the Literacies of Urban Youth*); and the urban community college campus with an open admissions policy—its students formerly academic outsiders, now moving from their worlds of work, to home, to school—underlie Ira Shor's calls for a critical pedagogy that works to transform social inequalities (*Critical Teaching and Everyday Life*). It is not hard to think of several other place-based writings and educational theories in composition and community literacy scholarship.

This discussion of community literacy work and place reminds us of how Anne Ruggles Gere drew attention to the "extracurricular"—or places beyond the university—where we find literacy at work. In her article, now over twenty years old, she writes, "They [writers] may gather in rented rooms in the Tenderloin, around kitchen tables in Lansing, Iowa, or in a myriad of other places to write their worlds. The question remains whether we will use classroom walls as instruments of separation or communication" (91). The answer, if I can be so bold as to claim one, is now here—the "extracurricular" is becoming the curricular as more educators are advocating for place-based literacies under names like service-learning, place-conscious education, ecocomposition and ecopedagogy, and urban and rural literacy studies. These subfields, of course, are not one in the same as they draw on scholarship from different disciplines with different methods and different ways of making (and counting) knowledge, and yet, there is a central theme here—the study of place as unveiling and shaping social and ecological reality.

Place-based literacies and their attention to how location creates possibilities for world-revealing and world-making practices, particularly in the sense of community development and literate practices, are now a dominant theme in pedagogy, community work, and scholarship. David Gruenewald, in his article "The Best of Both Worlds: A Critical Pedagogy of Place," offers a definition of the aims of place-based literacies that best describes its world-revealing and making potential when he writes that place pedagogies should "(a) identify, recover, and create material spaces and places that teach us how to live well in our total environments (reinhabitation); and (b) identify and change ways of thinking that injure and exploit other people and places (decolonization)" (9). These two aims are what he sees as the goals of place-based education (a) and critical pedagogy (b), and—as his title implies—he wishes for a convergence of these pedagogical approaches rather than to separate them. This synthesis is helpful because it accounts for how place is continually changing and how we need to be aware of and a part of this process. Just like in writing pedagogy, places also continually undergo a process of revision. As community literacy workers, we are in a position to understand and teach this process of revision to students and others so that they can (potentially) participate in acts of place-making.

Furthermore, when places are being revised, there is an impulse, like place-based educators argue, *to conserve*—the land, the culture, the local businesses, the local residents—and there is an impulse, like critical pedagogues argue, *to transform*, to make social reality better for those who have been traditionally marginalized or displaced (whether we are considering place as institution, place as neighborhood, place as city, or place as region). The dialectic of transformation and conservation is one that I want to trace through the scholarship of composition and community scholars when they write about and advocate for place-based literacies. This dialectic has a discourse, a rhetoric, one we must learn and deploy strategically, as compositionists and community literacy workers, in order to impact the lives of students and others with whom we work. In other words, sometimes we have to advocate for the conservation of a place and a current way of life, and other times we need to advocate for the transformation of a place and a new way of life. My intention, in analyzing the conservation and transformation dialectic in relation to this key phrase—place-based literacies—is to draw attention to how literacy work is a form of world-revealing and place-making.

Revision: The Conservation and Transformation of Places

Writing teachers and literacy workers are very cognizant of the revision process. As Adrienne Rich describes, writing is an act of re-vision "of looking-back, of seeing with fresh eyes" (18); revision is about perspective and we often teach our students to be open to envisioning what is not yet there. Revision is an imaginative labor. This section asks readers to consider our lens of revision in writing in relation to how we understand revision of place. This transference is an act of what Kenneth Burke calls "perspective by incongruity," a method that "gaug[es] situations by 'verbal atom cracking.' That is, a word belongs by custom to a certain category—and by rational planning you wrench it loose and metaphorically apply it to a different category" (308). Revision in writing studies holds complex meaning because it is associated with process pedagogies. We can think of the struggle over change that we see in our students' compositions, one where we observe how what is being revised retains elements of its original character or transforms into something entirely different. We offer feedback on this process. How is the process of revision in composition similar to that of revision of place?

There are many examples of scholars discussing revision of neighborhoods, landscapes, and campuses in community literacy and composition scholarship. For example, Jim W. Corder reflects often on the nature of revision (of writing, of place, of ourselves) as both a good and a bad thing. In one of his place-based memoirs, *Yonder: Life on the Far Side of Change*, he asks readers to see revision as inevitable, whether this inevitability is one of nature (erosion) or of human intervention (construction, interaction). In one passage he describes the Croton Breaks, a canyon in West Texas, as a case study of revision. The land has changed in Corder's lifetime because of wind, water, bulldozing, scraping, and leveling. He writes, "I recognize nothing when I go back," observing that this revision, "has torn the Canyons outside my knowledge and raped my care" (Yonder 90). Corder bristles at this revision of place, at revision in the writing process, at revision in life, insisting that "the first draft may be all I have" and questioning, "Might we take each other, and the other out there, without revision?" (91). And yet revision, and its inevitability, cannot be ignored or wished away. As Corder notes, revision is always already happening.

The dialectic of conservation and transformation is one we confront whenever we engage in a process of revision; for example, we may be shaping our ideas and putting them into words or deciding how to change our university's writing curricula or observing or participating in the construction of our landscapes and cityscapes. Revision is a part of engaging in the work of place-based literacies. We want to hold fast to some things, and we want to change some things; holding on and changing, of course, are sometimes out of our purview. Corder wrestles with this inevitability of revision through his remark, "Unrevised, I fail, of course, and get no credit in freshmen composition, or in life" (91). This remark could be read as fatalistic, but it could also be read as realistic. If we—as community literacy scholars and practitioners—note and participate in revision, maybe less will slip out of our purview? Maybe we can conserve what is good around us and we can transform what does not serve our communities? Place-making requires an attentiveness and a critical eye toward revision, and it requires us to be active participants in conservation and transformation.

Community literacy, as Rhonda Davis defines, is taking part in a process of "analyzing and learning from a matrix of *ever-evolving* relationships people and themselves, for better or worse, are embedded within" (emphasis mine, 80). This definition outlines literacy work as socially critical, ecological, and bound in processes of change. Our attention to how discourses form and shape social reality is at the heart of work in writing studies, but—as Nedra Reynolds articulates (See *Geographies of Writing*), scholars may be too focused on discourse. This focus may abstract the real issues and people behind the words, and also may make us less focused on the material conditions of literacy. For place is not a neutral backdrop for human action, a context for rhetorical activity and discourse; it greatly influences—and maybe even generates—communicative acts. In other words, place gives place to literacy practices. In this vein, Thomas Rickert argues in *Ambient Rhetoric* that the work of rhetoric (and literacy) is beyond human agents engaged in speech acts; he writes, that the study of rhetoric "must diffuse outward to include the material environment, things (including the technological), our own embodiment, and a complex understanding of ecological relationality as participating in rhetorical practices and their theorization" (3). We must continue to acknowledge the material dimension of rhetoric and literacy, to see it as an "embodied and embedded practice" (Rickert 34).

The practice of critical pedagogy and scholarship of place requires responsiveness to the dialectic of conservation and transformation. David Gruenewald argues that students "must be challenged to reflect on their own concrete situationality in a way that explores the complex interrelationships between cultural and ecological environments" (6). Being attentive to material conditions makes us aware of how places are changing. And we can respond to these changes—through our scholarship and in our literacy work—by investigating how communities develop in place, how identity development is tied to geography, how emotions circulate in place, how people become excluded through spatial organization, how the local community experiences loss through change, how physical movement (or lack of movement) is undertaken by bodies in place, and many other issues that concern us in the study of place-based literacies.

The following subsections elucidate different strands of work being done in place-based literacy: institutional and home literacies, urban and rural literacies, and eco-literacies. These divisions are made to showcase some of the different case studies and approaches scholars have taken in their recognition of place as a significant part of literacy practices. My aim is to see literacy work as a process of world-revealing and place-making, and further to see the scholarly writings reviewed here as a response to the ever-changing nature of places and the literacy practices that are created within them.

Institutional and Home Literacies

Boundary. This is one of many spatial metaphors to describe the place of basic writers in the academy. The scholarship of the basic writing movement in rhetoric and composition continually emphasizes the ways that students from nontraditional backgrounds are outsiders. Mike Rose's work on basic writers continues to resonate with composition and community literacy practitioners because he calls attention to the boundary lines, reminding us of the politics of remediation and the ways institutions are set up to displace basic writers (and, de facto, composition as a discipline) from the center of knowledge-making. Rose tries to arrive at a definition of remedial, and says it can be best described as "highly dynamic and contextual" in that labeling something as remedial in the university serves a function: "to keep in *place* the hard fought for, if historically and conceptually problematic and highly fluid, distinction between college and secondary work" (emphasis mine, 349). There is also a boundary that exists, both psychologically and materially, between what counts as knowledge in the academy and the ways of knowing and being that students learn through their home and work life experiences.

Much scholarship in community literacy and composition critiques the way power circulates in institutions and asks us to imagine how the boundary between institutional and home literacies can be less divisive. Institution as place is one site of analysis for place-based literacies. The division is indeed one that has caused oppression, perpetuating racial and class inequalities. Ira Shor defines critical literacy as a process of "questioning received knowledge and immediate experience" (11) in institutions, and for teachers to practice a pedagogy that "constructs students as authorities, agents, and unofficial teachers" (13) in order to empower them to return to their communities and become activists. Critical literacy, then, is situated in institutional and home communities—investigating these sites (and identifying and analyzing the social problems and asset-based epistemologies that circulate therein) is at the center of the curriculum. This approach to place-based literacies is one of transformation. For a further review of works in composition and community literacy scholarship that are critical of institutional organization and power, see Nedra Reynolds' *Geographies of Writing* as she traces spatial metaphors in the history of rhetoric and composition scholarship (Chapter 1); Glynda Hull and Katherine Schultz's *School's Out!: Bridging Out-of-School Literacies with Classroom Practice* as they provide a comprehensive overview of scholarship about out-of-school literacies through the frames of ethnography in education, Vygotskian and activity theory, and new literacy studies (Chapter 1); and Christopher J. Keller and Christian R. Weisser's edited collection, *The Locations of Composition*, particularly the writer contributions in Part III titled "Across the Institution."

It is important to note how the spatial metaphors to describe basic writers and teaching basic writing are not relics of a bygone time. Basic writers—and these issues in the academy—have not disappeared, even though some of our scholarly attention may have shifted away from them. A more contemporary article that engages issues of institution as place is Johnathon Mauk's "Location, Location, Location: The 'Real' (E)states of Being, Writing, and Thinking." Here Mauk explains a "contemporary" problem in the university; students, he claims, especially those in two-year colleges, are "unsituated in academic space." The university is not an "integral part" of who they are in the fact that they are not traditional academics (368). Furthermore, he says that many professors view their students as "as uninvolved, uninterested, and unmotivated" because they are too distracted from their studies by outside forces, like their "domestic, workplace, and recreational commitments" (370). The university or college, as place, competes with other locations in students' lives. Mauk claims that professors should not despair about the academic performance of the "new" student population, but rather professors should help students see the work of the academy as applicable to their everyday lives. Rather than "invit[ing] students to move into academic space," (386) professors should move academic space outward so that students can "conceive the space outside of the campus, outside of the classroom, as academic" (380). Although Mauk frames the current student population and their issues as "new," the student population described in older writings, even as far back as Mina Shaughnessy's *Errors and Expectations*, sounds eerily similar.

Mauk's writing, rather than advocating for the conservation of the academy, calls for its transformation, in the sense that students should view academic thinking as essential to their everyday lives. Mauk suggests that professors do this through their assignment design, creating assignments that ask students to reflect on their places, such as their neighborhoods, workplaces, and community organizations. By asking students to write about their locations outside school, professors place students within assignments and hopefully this will make them more engaged and critical about their everyday lives (379). Critical pedagogy, Nedra Reynolds contends, is part of composition's "imagined geography" (27) in that it is focused on the transformation of academic space in order to challenge boundaries present in the academy that serve to displace basic writers.

Urban and Rural Literacies

> So what about us? People want to gentrify Harlem, they don't care that this our home . . . Lots of us been here all our lives and you telling me somebody's gonna up and take it all away from our reach? Our home, neighbors, parks, even schools! This our home, where we belong.—Philip, *Harlem on Our Minds*

The changes occurring in urban and rural places due to economic development is a large part of what drives scholars in community literacy studies. Urban and rural literacy education helps students and community members respond critically to changes (i.e. gentrification) in order for people to have more agency in their lives.

Philip, a youth who participated in Columbia professor Valerie Kinloch's research, explains from his perspective how place—Harlem in this case—is a part of his identity and how the loss or change of place (due to gentrification) can be harmful to long-time residents. There is a strong sense in urban and rural literacy scholarship that the community should take back and reclaim public spaces. These efforts can be seen through the lens of conservation of place.

Linda Tolbert and Paul Theobald trace place-based education to Vygotskian ideas of social constructivism and Howard Gardner's multiple intelligences. They say that public schools need to create space for urban youth to "work with one another and discover something about the hardships they share living in America's passed-over urban places," and that this work will ultimately develop students' interpersonal and intrapersonal intelligences (Tolbert and Theobald 274). Discussing urban class and racial struggles is a part of schooling in a democratic society, one where students may go back to their home communities to work for the rights of people who live there. Tolbert and Theobald describe place-based pedagogy as a process of ". . . enculturation into an ethic of taking pride in one's ability to positively affect the quality of the shared space that a neighborhood represents" (273). Philip displays the pride that Tolbert and Theobald describe in his home, in where he belongs, and this sentiment translates into him taking action in Harlem; in Kinloch's book, for example, she describes how Philip and other youth attend fair housing meetings, protest Columbia University's expansion plans, and create new media texts that advocate for the conservation of places important to black culture. It is important to note how these efforts in neighborhood conservation constitute activism. As Tolbert and Theobald remind teachers, place-based education or service learning is not about "cleaning up a vacant lot," but rather connecting youth with their communities. As Robert Nistler and Angela Maiers describe, schools should provide "opportunities for family and social networks to be formed through activities in schools and communities" (9).

To move from theory of urban literacy to pedagogical practice, Valerie Kinloch's book *Harlem on Their Minds: Place, Race, and Literacies of Urban Youth* is a good resource (see chapter 4) and her article, "Literacy, Community, and Youth Acts of Place-Making," wherein she discusses how students create multimodal projects (i.e. writing, interviewing, videotaping) to address community issues and reach a wider audience with their texts. Lauren Esposito's "Where to Begin? Using Place-Based Writing to Connect Students with their Local Communities" discusses her experience teaching at the community college level in an urban location; she speaks about how she engages students to write about issues in their local communities by having them create public documents, in this case public service announcements (PSAs). Her guiding questions to student writers are particularly helpful, and she touches upon the conservation and transformation of place through them; Esposito writes: "What obligations do you have in these places and to/for whom are you responsible? What roles are you asked to perform and what roles do you choose to perform? Which aspects of these places should remain the same or change?" (72). These questions highlight the ethical responsibilities students may feel toward their communities and the ways they can choose to respond to them (or not); Esposito asks students to enter into a process of revision of their places through documenting change over time.

Scholars who write about rural literacies possess pedagogical strategies for teaching place-based writing and community projects that are worth reading as they explicitly engage students in reflecting on and imagining places. For example, Robert Brooke and Jason L. McIntosh discuss the concept of teaching "deep mapping," or having students identify landmarks of significance to them and then having them reflect on the communities and issues within these drawings; they argue that this "active conceptualization of space is a necessary prerequisite to writing *inside, in relationship to,* or *for* a place" (133). Furthermore, James S. Chisholm and Brandie Trent discuss digital storytelling as a way to engage students in exploring their communities; in particular, they show an example of a student's photo essay and explain her composing process. They write that digital storytelling gave this student "the opportunity to learn deeply about narrative composition; to author her story, experiment with notions of identity, home, stability, change, and memory; and, finally, to connect these intellectual insights with the emotion that connects these concepts with place" (Chisholm and Trent 315). Both pedagogical articles emphasize the role of emotion for students in connection with their places and also encourage teachers and literacy workers to draw out these reflections in writing and visual projects.

There are also many articles written by educators that encourage place-based pedagogical strategies in teacher preparation programs, specifically for educating students from rural areas (See Ajayi, Eppley, Lester, Lesley and Matthews). Again, these pedagogical strategies are framed through the lens of conservation of rural values. Ajayi's definition of place-based literacies in teacher preparation is instructive here, as he writes that this pedagogy "connect[s] ELA [English Language Arts] to contextual realities of rural communities" and allows student-teachers to "appreciate what is locally vibrant within the community" helping them "to sustain and preserve" cultural practices and to approach community members as resources and partners in every aspect of teaching and learning (252). Many of the above articles emphasize how teacher preparation curriculum should become more place-based so that teachers can better relate to their students' lives and further engage their imaginations around issues of place-making. There is a real sense, too, that these students will return to their communities and become advocates for their preservation in the face of economic change.

The scholarship in both urban and rural literacies emphasizes community resources, which are found in the natural surroundings, the local culture, and in the actual members of the community. This asset-based framing for pedagogy and scholarship is one step toward arguing for the conservation of urban and rural places and communities.

Eco-literacies

Place-based literacies are also constructed through the use of metaphors—like network and web—that describe the relationship between people and their environments. These images of place show how it is ecological, constructed of human and non-human elements that continue to influence, or act on and with, each other. For an extensive discussion of the term *ecology*, it is important to reference Janine Morris' recent keyword essay in *Community Literacy Journal* as she characterizes ecologies as having a "reciprocal nature" that accounts for the "distribution, influence, and movement of organisms within and between environments" (89). Rhonda Davis, author of "A Place for Ecopedagogy in Community Literacy," adds to this definition as she works to define ecopedagogy; she writes that ecopedagogy recognizes the "reciprocal relationship that involves other people, nonhuman others, the natural environment, and constructed environments" (81). The use of *reciprocal* as an adjective in both these articles here is important because it emphasizes how scholars in this particular area of place-based literacies want to ensure that the environment (natural and built) is seen as a key player in the formation of literacy practices. We can see these ecological theories of composition and literacy as a posthuman response; literacy doesn't just reside in us, but rather is created and distributed across several actors.

Eco-literacies attempt to map the relationships between people, discourse, and place. Scholars in ecocomposition emphasize how writing always comes from somewhere, that discourse is not some detached entity. Discourse is created through relationships with place that are a "deeply enmeshed, coconstitutive relationship" (Dobrin 18). Sidney Dobrin asserts, "It is difficult, if not impossible, to separate the writing from the place and the place from the writing" (18). Further, Dobrin asserts that writers are as a "part of the web" as we are influenced by context: "it reverberates within us and we reverberate in it. There is no way not to affect the environment and be affected by it" (21). Eco-literacies constantly remind us how our characters and identities are created through place; place shapes us, and we shape it. Indeed, eco-literacies ask for scholars and community literacy workers to be aware of relationships and revisions that occur in ecosystems. This is a part of the *transformation* of place: as human agents, we are one variable in this process of transformation.

For pedagogical application of eco-literacies, see Paul Walker's article "(Un)earthing a Vocabulary of Values: A Discourse Analysis for Ecocomposition." Walker offers an analytical method through which "students engage in 'discursive ecology' by exploring the connections among discourse, people, and the environment with the intent to 'produce writing' that addresses those contextual connections (Dobrin and Weisser 116–17)" (Walker 70). Through a local case study, whether or not to expand Arizona's Snowbowl ski resort, Walker helps students analyze the discourses of various stakeholders (Native American tribes who argue the land is sacred and the owners of the resort who recommend expansion) in order to see how people understand and discuss their relationship with place. For further reference on eco-literacies in pedagogy, please see Derek Owen's *Composition and Sustainability: Teaching for a Threatened Generation* and several contributions in Dobrin and Weisser's edited collection, *Ecocomposition: Theoretical and Pedagogical Approaches*.

Place-based literacies are essential to our composition curricula and community literacy work. Place-based literacies help us understand how place is central to literacy practices and our theories about those practices. Being attentive to place allows scholars, students, and community members to discuss how places matter and are essential identity. This attentiveness also reveals how places change over time. I believe Gruenewald's idea of eco-justice should be the aim of our pedagogical and community practice; as educators and community workers, we must "develop an ethic of social and ecological justice where issues of race, class, gender, language, politics, and economics must be worked out in terms of people's relationship to their total environments, human and non-human" (6). The revision of place is inevitable, but we are ever reminded that we can participate in this change through our advocacy for the conservation and transformation of places in order to better our social realities.

Works Cited

Ajayi, Laisi. "Investigating Effective Teaching Methods for a Place-Based Teacher Preparation in a Rural Community." *Education Research Policy and Practice*. 13 (2014): 251–268.

Brooke, Robert and Jason L. McIntosh. "Deep Maps: Teaching Rhetorical Engagement Through Place-Conscious Education." *The Locations of Composition*. Ed. Christopher J. Keller and Christian R. Weisser. Albany: State University of New York P, 131–149.

Burke, Kenneth. *Attitudes Toward History*. 3rd Ed. University of California P, 1984.

Chisholm, James S. and Brandie Trent. "Digital Storytelling in a Place-Based Composition Course." *Journal of Adolescent and Adult Literacy*. 57.4 (Dec 2013 / Jan 2014): 307–318.

Corder, Jim W. *Yonder: Life on the Far Side of Change*. Athens: University of Georgia P, 1992.

Davis, Rhonda. "A Place for Ecopedagogy in Community Literacy." *Community Literacy Journal*. 7.2 (Spring 2013). 77–91.

Dobrin, Sidney. "Writing Takes Place." *Ecocomposition: Theoretical and Pedagogical Approaches*. Ed. Christian R. Weisser and Sidney I. Dobrin. Albany, New York: State University of New York P, 2001. 11–25.

Eppley, Karen. "Teaching Rural Place: Pre-Service Language and Literacy Students Consider Place-Conscious Literacy." *Pedagogies: An International Journal.* 6.2 (April–June 2011): 87–103.

Esposito, Lauren. "Where to Begin? Using Place-Based Writing to Connect Students with their Local Communities." *English Journal.* 101.4 (2012): 70–76.

Freire, Paolo. *Pedagogy of the Oppressed.* New York: Seabury, 1970.

Gere, Anne Ruggles. "Kitchen Tables and Rented Rooms: The Extracurriculum of Composition." *College Composition and Communication.* 45.1 (Feb., 1994): 75–92.

Gruenewald, David. "The Best of Both Worlds: A Critical Pedagogy of Place." *Educational Researcher.* 32.4 (2003): 3–12.

Keller, Christopher J. and Christian R. Weisser. *The Locations of Composition.* Albany:State University of New York P, 251–265.

Kinloch, Valerie. *Harlem on Our Minds: Place, Race, and the Literacies of Urban Youth.* New York: Teachers College P, 2010.

_____. "Literacy, Community, and Youth Acts of Place-Making." *English Education.* 41.4 (July 2009): 316–336.

Lesley, Mellinee and Marian Matthews. "Place-Based Essay Writing and Content Area Literacy Instruction for Preservice Teachers." *Journal of Adolescent & Adult Literacy.* 52.6 (2009): 523–33.

Mauk, Johnathon. "Location, Location, Location: The 'Real'(E)states of Being, Writing,and Thinking in Composition." *College English.* 65.4 (2003): 368–388.

Morris, Janine. "Ecology." *Community Literacy Journal.* 9.2 (2015): 85–91.

Nistler, Robert and Angela Maiers. "Exploring Home-School Connections: A Family Literacy Perspective on Improving Urban Schools." *Education and Urban Society.* 32.1 (November 1999): 3–17.

Owens, Derek. *Composition and Sustainability: Teaching for a Threatened Generation.* Urbana, Illinois: National Council of Teachers of English, 2001.

Rich, Adrienne. "When We Dead Awaken: Writing as Re-Vision." *College English.* 34.1 (Oct., 1972): 18–30.

Rickert, Thomas. *Ambient Rhetoric: The Attunements of Rhetorical Being.* PA:University of Pittsburgh P, 2013. Print.

Reynolds, Nedra. *Geographies of Writing: Inhabiting Places and Encountering Difference.* Carbondale: Southern Illinois, 2004. Print.

Rose, Mike. "The Language of Exclusion: Writing Instruction at the University." *College English.* 47.4 (Apr., 1985): 341–59.

_____. *Lives on the Boundary: A Moving Account of the Struggles and Achievements of America's Educationally Underprepared.* Penguin, 2005.

Rural Voices: Place Conscious Education and the Teaching of Writing. Ed. Robert Brooke. New York: Teachers College P, 2003.

School's Out!: Bridging Out-of-School Literacies and Classroom Practice. Ed. Glynda Hull and Katherine Schultz. New York: Teachers College P, 2002.

Shaughnessy, Mina. *Errors and Expectations: A Guide for the Teacher of Basic Writing.* London: Oxford UP, 1979.

Shor, Ira. *Critical Teaching and Everyday Life.* University of Chicago P, 1987.

_____. "What is Critical Literacy?" *Journal of Pedagogy, Pluralism, and Practice.* 1.4 (1999): n.p.

Tolbert, Linda and Paul Theobald. "Finding Their Place In the Community: Urban Education Outside the Classroom." *Childhood Education.* (2006): 271–274.

Walker, Paul. "(Un)earthing a Vocabulary of Values: A Discourse Analysis for Ecocomposition." *Composition Studies.* 38.1 (2010): 69–87.

Writing Our Way Out: Memoirs From Jail
Edited by David Coogan

Richmond: Brandylane P, 2016. 243 pp.

Reviewed by Maria Conti
University of Arizona

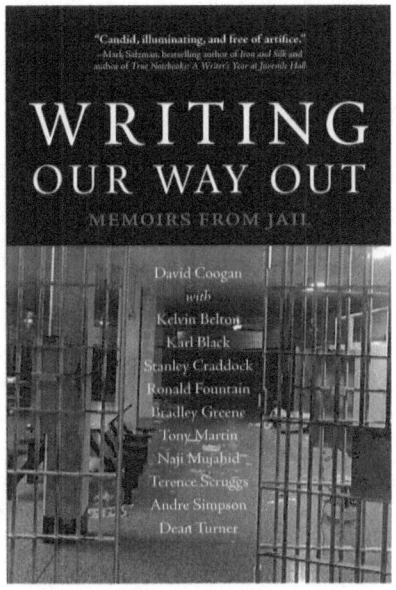

[Life is] about discovering the beauty that lies dormant inside of your fellow human beings. It's about giving love and then receiving it . . . . When you look at me, you won't see any of the above, at least not on the outside of who I appear to be. But x-ray me with your mind. Listen to my words. Look into my eyes. Here, let me help you. You'll need a light, because it's dark in my world . . . . You'll see the prison inside me (191).

—Stan, writing workshop participant

Prison writing program facilitators Wendy Wolters Hinshaw and Tobi Jacobi explain that while the public is inundated with fictional depictions of incarcerated people, we are not often able to hear from them directly ("What Words" 68). David Coogan's *Writing Our Way Out: Memoirs from Jail* offers readers this rare opportunity. As creative nonfiction, the majority of the book is comprised of the intimate reflections of ten incarcerated writers. The epigraph above is a microcosm of the raw, honest exploration of self that echoes throughout the piece. What makes the work even more insightful for both instructors in carceral settings and writing teachers is that Coogan includes his own memoir of teaching at the Richmond City Jail.[1] He begins each chapter with a first-person account of what he is thinking at different stages in the project. Rich in dialogue from the workshop and Coogan's inner monologue, these interludes provide context for the stories to come.

A scholar of rhetoric as social change whose work is familiar to many *CLJ* readers, Coogan makes a connection between this book and community-engaged research and praxis. Notably, he frames the project with Michael Warner's theory of the counterpublic, a term originally coined by Nancy Fraser. Counterpublics provide discursive space for people excluded from the dominant power structure of the mainstream public sphere. Coogan asks, "Given that prisoners have been effectively sidelined from public life by their incarceration, how are we to hear their voices—that sound of their citizen-selves becoming?" (2). Indeed, incarcerated people usually have restricted access to online participation in the public sphere that would enable this exercise of citizenship. A central feature of Coogan's epistemological stance is his belief that grassroots projects can affect publics in meaningful ways, "ris[ing] like beanstalks into the hard-to-reach public spheres of empathy, insight, and inclusiveness that were typically obscured by all of the rants, ignorance, and stale air below" (11). In other words, projects emerging from the ground up have the potential to transcend the empty, unproductive rhetoric often present in discussions about incarceration.

The hope of the writing class was "that each man might understand the story of his life, and in so doing, change its course" (xi). Despite his grand vision, the book does not indulge in the self-congratulatory rhetoric of 'this-is-what-I-did-look-how-great-it-is.' Rather, Coogan honestly communicates the unique frustrations and administrative stumbling blocks that come with teaching in a jail. At times, he questioned whether the workshop would be able to continue due to the sudden transfer of participants to other facilities. The first eleven chapters take place during the workshop's first year at the Richmond City Jail. Because many of the original participants were transferred, the project continued via letters. The final eight chapters follow the men in prison and their lives afterwards, between 2008 and 2011.

Chapter 1, "A World You Used to Live In," details the first meeting at the jail. Coogan delineates four categories that will serve as the "narrative arc" of each man's story: the *past* (people from your childhood, your neighborhood), the *problem* (when you started to get into trouble), the *punishment* (facts of your crime(s), your emotional reaction), and the *possibilities* (ambitions for the future, what you can offer others) (10–11). Many of the stories blend into each other across individual lives as they discuss experiences with substance abuse, addiction, sexuality, childhood abuse, remorse, police brutality, religion, education, family, and change. These compelling anecdotes moved me and stayed with me long after I finished the book. Strong sensory details place the reader in the scenes, which read like excerpts from a novel. The work as a whole has the feel of a bricolage, as the narrative moves from one writer's story to another within each chapter.

Even though the workshop focuses on personal, reflective writing, it leaves room for incarcerated participants to move toward critical literacy. Hinshaw and Jacobi point out that programs are often overly focused on individual rehabilitation at the expense of other approaches that the writers might want to engage, such as systemic critique (72–73). Throughout the book, participants describe elements of their environment that contributed to their involvement in criminal activity. One especially poignant story that leads the reader toward systemic critique is Brad's. He turns himself in to the police, reasoning, "I would rather go and do twenty years in prison than to keep living the way I'm living!" (217). The fact that Brad perceives prison as a safer place than the rest of his world speaks to the lack of options for many incarcerated people. Others, such as Dean, reflect on the challenges post-incarceration in light of limited access to employment, housing, and transportation: "There have been so many times when I wanted so badly to change the way I lived and my way of thinking. . . . I needed money (no job). I needed a place to stay that I could call my own (not enough money). I needed a better-paying job (no car)" (215). In Chapter 14, "My Story Is Still Being Told," Ronald also describes the difficulty of breaking free from the cycle of incarceration: "I have no clue how to manifest a change. All I know is that I must find the way to wholeness" (172). Statements such as these help readers to understand the revolving door of incarceration, release, and recidivism.

The workshop participants also employ analogies between the criminal justice system and institutions of U.S. slavery. In Chapter 15, "The Prison Inside Me," Kelvin names elements of being incarcerated that are similar to the situation of a slave on a plantation. In both slavery and incarceration, people are sold or are being sold out by members of their own community (192). Both groups of people are made to work for little or no pay (193). The most significant comparison in Kelvin's extended analogy for educators and writing teachers may be his discussion of slaves and incarcerated people as they reenter society. Kelvin explains that, like recently-freed slaves, "most inmates lack the knowledge and understanding it takes to survive" (194). Because participants are given discursive space to move beyond the personal, they have the opportunity to critique the severely flawed systems that govern their daily lives. Readers of this work benefit from these insider perspectives on the types of support that are most needed.

In Chapter 16, "Dreams of Change," Karl and Naji write about the factors that make it difficult to succeed in carceral settings, such as little or no access to educational programs, computers, library materials, life skills classes, and counselors (200, 207, 210). In light of these issues, Naji began to see his drug addiction in a "much broader context": " . . . not only am I a perpetrator, but I'm a victim as well. I'm not a victim of a drug culture that fell upon me somehow, leaving me without any choices—I'm more like a victim of a system out of control, one that profits off the unfortunate mistakes and bad decisions I have made" (210). The gaps in programming and resources that participants identify can provide points of entry for educators interested in working with incarcerated writers.

One of the high points of the book, in my view, is that Coogan's memoir addresses positionality and social location issues for instructors in detention centers, jails, and prisons. He demonstrates how the participants' worlds are strikingly different than his own in several ways. At one point, Kelvin recalls that Coogan was the first person who asked him when he knew what he really wanted out of life. Coogan reflects, "In a flash I recall how many times I answered that question—what I *wanted* to do—from family and teachers when I was in high school" (56). He goes on to wonder what it would be like not to have that guiding question in his life (56). Despite differences in social location, Coogan was asked by Dean to be his mentor in a program for ex-offenders, and he was subpoenaed as a character witness for Andre's trial. These examples illustrate how people from the outside often have comparative social power.

In acknowledgement of this power differential, Coogan engages in a set of ethical best practices throughout the project.[2] For example, he purposely did not read background information offered to him about the participants' crimes. This distancing allows the writers to reveal this information when they are ready. Secondly, all participants gave final approval for the way their writing appears in the book, and they were given the option of using a pseudonym. In a consent form, Coogan also made it clear that the writers could stop participating at any time. Notably, workshop participation did not obligate them to publish in the book. These measures provide opportunities for agency and indicate a profound respect for participants. Finally, Coogan and the writers made publication decisions together. In opposition to a top-down model in which the program facilitator decides how and when the stories enter the public sphere, publication with an academic press was a collective decision. As more people venture into the uncharted territory of carceral writing, it is clear that we need to think carefully about power and ethical practices. This work offers a crucial step in the right direction.

The writing workshop has been succeeded by Open Minds, a program Coogan founded in 2010, that enables incarcerated people to take courses with college students and faculty from Virginia Commonwealth University. In addition, Coogan invites former participants of the project to speak in his prison literature classes. These approaches, along with *Writing Our Way Out*, are critical for countering monolithic conceptions of people who are incarcerated. The stereotypes circulating in the public sphere are counterproductive to the shift in public opinion needed for meaningful intervention in the broken U.S. criminal justice system. As a counterpublic text, this book provides a valuable blueprint for scholars, educators, and activists to become part of the intervention, and ultimately, the solution.

Endnotes

1. While referring to Coogan by his last name and the workshop participants by their first names might suggest a hierarchical relationship, I have chosen to use the participants' first names, as is done throughout the book.

2. For a more detailed discussion of ethical best practices with incarcerated writers, see Hinshaw and Jacobi (2015).

Works Cited

Hinshaw, Wendy Wolters and Tobi Jacobi. "What Words Might Do: The Challenge of Representing Women in Prison and Their Writing." *Feminist Formations* 27.1 (2015): 67–90. *Project Muse: Premium Collection*. Web. 17 Nov. 2015.

Toward a Literacy of Promise: Joining the African American Struggle
Edited by Linda A. Spears-Bunton and Rebecca Powell

New York: Routledge, 2009. 208 pp.

Reviewed by Anthony Dwayne Boynton, II
Georgia College & State University

Linda Spears-Bunton and Rebecca Powell's anthology of essays is an invitation to literacy activists to stand up for the education of historically marginalized communities and a guide of culturally relevant pedagogy for the teachers fatigued by the monotony of the canon. The teacher-scholars featured in *Toward a Literacy of Promise* not only ask us to consider joining in this culturally responsive pedagogy, a literacy of promise, but offer us a comprehensive look at the challenges marginalized groups have faced in classrooms while bestowing feasible solutions to the archaic demands of historically conservative pedagogy. Readers of *Community Literacy Journal* will thoroughly enjoy this text for it is seminal for any teacher engaging with millennial students. The essayists mark this generation as new readers of everything, of texts, images, their lives and society, critically defining literacy as an engagement and the "ability to function in the world" (152). The literacy of promise is a hope toward a more whole and liberal, truly liberating, education and classroom.

This text is organized well, containing a foreword by Lisa Delpit, an introduction by Rebecca Powell, and then three sections that work as a pathway to progressive education in the 21st century. Each of the ten chapters end in discussion questions to reflect on and further the chapter's details and activities that bring theory and practice to the fore.

Powell's introduction, chapter one, defines the literacy of promise as "a literacy that potentially empowers students and teachers and that gives them a voice. A literacy of promise requires students to negotiate meaning and to be actively engaged in discerning relationships of power and repression in society" (xiii). Literacy here is magnified conceptually beyond simply reading the written word; instead, literacy— as a concept—invites learners of all kinds to read their lives and experiences as ones influenced by power relations. The readers are asked to be critical of these relationships and use the literacy of promise to rethink or reroute their practices.

The first section is entitled "Problems and Promises"—herein the writers delineate societal and historical situations where literacy plays an integral role and how a literacy of promise is able to counteract these problems. The second chapter, entitled "Along the Road to Social Justice: a Literacy of Promise," is written by the two editors, leading the way to understanding the critical nature of literacy. Spears-Bunton and Powell find literacy to be a catalyst toward gaining cultural capital—a major contributor to the power and privileges to write, change, enforce, and amend rules and laws that govern societies. Throughout the text, the writers focus on how schools and classrooms are appropriate spaces to dismantle these powers that have been historically reserved to certain classes and bestow voice to all. The literacy of promise "intentionally presents a challenge to the status quo" (23), which is illustrated in questioning the texts we teach and the presumptions we make about students of color.

There is a history of what schools have deemed acceptable in terms of speech, writing, and study. Spears-Bunton and Powell inform us that conservative and ill-functioning pedagogy, which they name schooled literacies—an older canon of methods and books by writers who are not culturally relevant to underrepresented groups (these writers are normally upper-class, white, cisgendered men)—enforce hierarchies of power. These hierarchies distance power away from oppressed groups, deeming them unreliable to engage or manage their space and voice in the classroom and society. Teachers must assess the validity of multicultural (and countercultural) texts if they are willing to join in the literacy of promise and African American struggle, for it is through those texts that the literacy of promise can "give rise to social consciousness" and transcend "the boundaries of class, race, gender, ignorance, hopelessness and learned helplessness" (37).

Spears-Bunton and Powell ask educators and activists to question their assumptions about a multicultural canon, non-mainstream literacies, and the spectrum of language acquisition skills. Literacy is learned and performed in and outside of the classroom and understanding how to teach students to apply those literacies in and outside of the classroom will benefit them to a greater degree than teaching material that is not relevant to their experiences. Spears-Bunton and Powell conclude the chapter by stating their mission, which is lifetime occupation of working with *all* people "along the road toward social justice" (37). The "all" is demonstrated well in the following chapters, where the writers, from a number of disciplines and backgrounds, execute different case studies and strategies that work toward the literacy of promise.

Chapter 3 asserts reformation is needed in multicultural literacy classrooms. Written by Letita Hochstrasser Fickel, "'Unbanking' Education" discusses what unbanking practices look like within literacy classrooms. She critiques the conventional classroom for its omniscient professor who lords over the feeble-minded student. This kind of class reiterates and solidifies a hierarchal power structure and makes for passive regurgitators of information as well as rendering a multiplicity of cultural experiences and learning styles irrelevant. Fickel reframes the classroom as a space where all are learners and teachers simultaneously. Students, under the mandate of the literacy of promise, are asked to be active and forward-thinking critics of the world around them. This ideology is based on Paulo Freire's *Pedagogy of the Oppressed* and *The Politics of Education* where he recommends students study the world critically rather than simply living *in* it uncritically.

Fickel's chapter relies heavily on the work of Freire, almost too much so. While Freire's work is definitely seminal to anyone who works in the convergence zone of academia and social justice, this chapter is too dependent on Freire's work. The exploration of Freire's work, via several theoretical frameworks, ultimately allowed for greater analysis wherein Fickel could lay bare her own thoughts on liberating education for African American classrooms where everyday texts, magazines, commercials, music videos, etc., can be used to examine one's life and society toward the aim of critical literacy.

Chapter 4 completes and compliments the first section well. Spears-Bunton writes with Sherman G. Helenese and Kimberly L. Bunton in chapter 4, titled "Resistance, Reading, Writing, and Redemption: Defining Moment in Literacy and the Law," to both complete and compliment the first section of the book. This chapter is a timely call for educators to understand the high stakes of reading, writing, and literacy for historically underprivileged communities. This is a chapter in which teachers of English, history, political science, and sociology will be most interested. The scholars featured in this chapter argue that there is a "symbiotic relationship between literacy and the law" (57). Literacy in the U.S. functions as a humanizing force and a vehicle for political participation and citizenry. The authors suggest that the struggle for literacy is related to the quest for "human dignity, efficacy, and authenticity" (59). Throughout the chapter, the writers explore laws and policies that have adversely impacted the political participation of people of color in America from Reconstruction through the Civil Rights Movement. This historical mapping is accomplished in not only naming and asserting the power of legal exclusion over oppressed groups, but also in stating the reality of discrimination and what social activists have accomplished to counter the hegemonic force of unjust laws. Spears-Bunton, Helenese, and Bunton complete this chapter with a literacy test that can be used to demonstrate these realities and for discussion of the critical nature of literacy and democratic participation.

In the section titled "Realizing a Literacy of Promise through Literary Texts" and the two chapters therein, the authors do not make the case for their argument using texts that are often employed in writing classrooms. While this may seem like a problem at first glance, the point of the literacy of promise is to incorporate and analyze unconventional texts from multiple perspectives, so the writers of this section are in good keeping with the thematic concerns Spears-Bunton and Powell make manifest. Introducing and juxtaposing these new(er) voices against the continuum of schooled literacy is a constructive and smart move.

Julia Johnson-Connor and Arlette Ingram Willis wrote chapter 5, "'Educational, Controversial, Provocative, and Personal': Three African American Adolescent Males Reflect on Critical Framing *A Lesson Before Dying*." Within the chapter, Johnson-Connor and Willis interview three of their students, using their responses to Ernest Gaines' novel and stories about school experiences as the focus for the chapter. This makes for an honest narrative where the students can express their relationship to writing, literature, and social justice. Johnson-Connor and Willis preface the students' stories with how they conceptualized a "Minority Authors" elective course that focuses on African American texts and then share some of the assumptions faculty colleagues have on the subject of teaching beyond the canon. They interview three male students, Vincent, Ahmad, and Clarence, before and after reading *A Lesson Before Dying*, and charted the differences between the students' answers to questions about the text. They were specifically questioned about their definition or vision of a "perfect world" and before reading Gaines' text, the answers were not engaged or thoughtful at all about their world(s) or life. There was a marked difference in their answers after reading, one that seemed to contend with how race and discrimination affected their lives.

Chapter 6 is a call for white female teachers to consider using multiple perspectives and multicultural texts. Spears-Bunton's "The Obscured White Voice in the Multicultural Debate: Race, Space, and Gender" investigates Paula's classroom. The teacher asks compelling rhetorical questions at the outset of the chapter: "What happens to a Black kid who never gets to read a book written by a Black author? How do the White kids feel about the emphasis on Black literature?" (106). Paula's questions about difference and curriculum is a double-edged sword. Her school had a subtle mandate to avoid racial topics, but Paula found this kind of monocultural teaching unacceptable in that it enforces cultural blindspots and ignorance about the world in which we live.

Spears-Bunton's initial questions, in chapter 6, lead the reader to believe that the chapter will focus on Black students' experiences with Black texts (perhaps for the first time) in the classroom. However, Spears-Bunton refocuses the question toward white students' first time experiences with Black texts. She does this in order to demonstrate how multicultural texts can have a culturally relevant and positive impact on all students. White students complete interviews in order to demonstrate and expand their understanding about how distance and difference work in white students' engagement in texts from other cultural groups. Bridging these gaps are a large part of the literacy of promise, as the writer reminds us in the conclusion of the chapter, "Moving toward a literacy of promise is not without risk. . . . [S]ilence does not resolve cultural ambiguity, contradiction or conflict;" in fact, silence may lead to further conflict (119–20). The third section of chapter 6, "Realizing a Literacy of Promise through Oral and Popular Texts," Spears-Bunton exhibits how the millennial student and teacher can engage in critical literacies and create supportive educational environments for students from historically oppressed and marginalized groups.

The often-fought battle of Black English's place in the classroom is fought by Ira Kincade Blake in chapter 7, "Ebonics and the Struggle for Cultural Voice in U.S. Schools." While this chapter can be used to assess high school students' silence and voice, she posits that a study of elementary schools is necessary to chart cultural voice in the classroom. All children, she claims, come to school equipped with their home languages, what she calls "the cultural backpack" (139). Once they enter school, these home languages are placed into categories of acceptability; school then becomes a cultural battleground that creates borders for what is worth voicing and in whose dialect. The results of this are often Standard English registers are embraced as Black English speech is shut down. Blake argues that language is raced and classed and that schools create and police students differently. Blake extends this analysis by asking the reader to recall George W. Bush's presidency and his linguistic performances. The chapter examines how Bush's race and class allow for protection of his status and title despite his "bad" English. Blake ultimately asks us all to make classrooms and schools that are supportive of the differences in linguistic performance and standards of communication across cultures.

Jessica S. Bryant's chapter "The Potential of Oral Literacy for Empowerment" pairs well with Blake's immediately prior chapter. This thoughtful chapter-by-chapter organization gives a holistic picture of how orality should be a focus within our classrooms. Bryant uses Blake's conclusion to discuss how to make supportive classroom spaces, asking us to disrupt the history of teachers-as-gatekeepers-of-knowledge convention that is often seen in classrooms across the country, in different disciplines, from elementary to secondary and higher education. This chapter invites us to make a student-centered classroom where students feel free to discuss and engage in the topics at hand. This kind of classroom makes for better thinkers and readers who critically discern their lives and opinions, instead of merely rehearsing what has been told to them.

Chapter nine is compelling in that the writer's execution of the literacy of promise is not only one that is performed in the classroom, but also on stage. Karen B. McLean Donaldson writes "Voices of Our Youth: Antiracist Social Justice Theater Arts Makes a Difference in the Classroom" to describe the ways she has used her dramatic arts expertise to invoke the literacy of promise for students who have dealt with racial tension in their schools. Donaldson has worked all over the U.S. and focuses on two specific occasions in inner-city schools where she could instantly tell her students were impacted by the systemic racism. In each of her productions, she asks her students to write and perform spoken word poems and skits that embody how to interpret their relationship to social justice. Donaldson has students enact a literacy of promise on stage that she hopes will extend to their daily lives (172).

The tenth and final chapter by Rebecca Powell enlarges the literacy of promise to "The Promise of Critical Media Literacy". Powell invites teachers to consider moving beyond the written word in this chapter. Powell cites popular culture as a space that millennial students will engage in their daily lives and will need to reflect critically upon. She says hip-hop, fashion, film, and advertisements are clear representatives of one's socio-political context and world (189). The writer examines the movies *Black Barbie* and *Baby Boy* in order to discern their worth as multicultural texts to be examined in the classroom. She concludes with a call to arms to English teachers, but I find that this call is for "all" teachers to make important choices about including non-traditional texts in order to have enable transformative classroom experiences.

Toward a Literacy of Promise offers provocative suggestions for teachers interested in literacy studies and clearly aspires to reach a wide cross-disciplinary audience. Spears-Bunton and Powell's edited collection challenges readers to think about relationships between language, identity, power, community, subjectivity, pedagogy, literature, and critical literacy. Their work calls scholars and teachers to acknowledge and respect the differences that create human diversity and variability in experiencing, understanding, composing, and critiquing the world. Overall, practitioners and theorists of critical literacy will benefit from the essays in this well-written and well-researched anthology.

DEPAUL UNIVERSITY

DEPARTMENT OF
WRITING, RHETORIC, & DISCOURSE

Master of Arts Degrees in
NEW MEDIA STUDIES
WRITING, RHETORIC, & DISCOURSE
with concentrations in
Professional & Technical Writing
Teaching Writing & Language

Graduate certificate in TESOL
Combined BA/MA in WRD

Bachelor of Arts in **WRITING, RHETORIC, & DISCOURSE**
Minor in **Professional Writing**

 facebook.com/DePaulWRD   @DePaulWRD

WRD.DEPAUL.EDU

PARLOR PRESS
EQUIPMENT FOR LIVING

Congratulations to These Award Winners & WPA Scholars!

The WPA Outcomes Statement—A Decade Later
   Edited by Nicholas N. Behm, Gregory R. Glau, Deborah H. Holdstein, Duane Roen, and Edward M. White
   Winner of the Best Book Award, Council of Writing Program Adminstrators (July, 2015)

GenAdmin: Theorizing WPA Identities in the Twenty-First Century
   Colin Charlton, Jonikka Charlton, Tarez Samra Graban, Kathleen J. Ryan, & Amy Ferdinandt Stolley
   Winner of the Best Book Award, Council of Writing Program Adminstrators (July, 2014)

Mics, Cameras, Symbolic Action: Audio-Visual Rhetoric for Writing Teachers
   Bump Halbritter
   Winner of the Distinguished Book Award from Computers and Composition (May, 2014)

New Releases

A Rhetoric for Writing Program Administrators, 2nd ed.
   Edited by Rita Malenczyk

A Critical Look at Institutional Mission: A Guide for Writing Program Administrators
   Edited by Joseph Janangelo

Play/Write: Digital Rhetoric, Writing, Games Digital Rhetoric, Writing, Games'
   Edited by Douglas Eyman and Andréa D. Davis

First-Year Composition: From Theory to Practice
   Edited by Deborah Coxwell-Teague & Ronald F. Lunsford

www.parlorpress.com

www.ingramcontent.com/pod-product-compliance
Lightning Source LLC
Chambersburg PA
CBHW031601170426
43196CB00032B/1014